YOU'RE GOING TO BE A DAD!

ADAM, LEWIS AND SKYE

ALEX AND RAFFI

AMEET AND HARJOT

AMISH

BEN AND BARNABY

COLE AND MAISEY

DAMIAN AND GRACE

DAVID

FIELD AND CYRUS

FRED

JANEK AND DAUGHTER

JASON AND FINLEY

JON AND DAUGHTER

KEITH AND STELLEN

KENEAL AND DAUGHTER

KRISTOPHER AND SON

LEE AND DAUGHTER

LOUIS

MARK AND JAMIE

MASON AND MAX

MATTEO AND JACK

ROB AND SON

WE'VE INTERVIEWED DADS AND DADS-TO-BE FROM ALL ACROSS THE WORLD TO BRING YOU A DIVERSE RANGE OF INSIGHTS AND LEARNINGS. SOME OF THEM ARE PROFILED HERE THAT YOU WILL READ ABOUT FIRSTHAND.

A MASSIVE THANK YOU TO ALL OF THEM.

ROBIN AND DYLAN

ROY AND VERITY

ROYCE AND JALEN

SIMON AND GOLDIE

WILLIAM AND MICA

ZIKO AND AMAIA

TWO SPECIAL GIFTS FOR OUR READERS

AS A SPECIAL THANK YOU FOR GETTING THIS BOOK, WE'D LIKE TO GIVE YOU:

HOW TO SURVIVE ON 3 HOURS SLEEP A DAY

THE SPECIFIC TIPS AND INSIGHTS FROM THE EXPERTS ON HOW THEY SURVIVE ON VERY LITTLE SLEEP.

+

HOW TO CHOOSE YOUR BABY'S NAME

DON'T JUST RELY ON A LIST OF NAMES. LEARN ABOUT A MUCH WIDER RANGE OF NAMING TECHNIQUES TO GET TO A NAME YOU AND YOUR PARTNER WILL LOVE!

VISIT WWW.DADDILIFE.COM/NEWDADGOODS TO GET YOURS!

TABLE OF CONTENTS

INTRODUCTION

"We're going to have a baby. You're going to be a dad!"

The world slows down. You make sure you heard that right. They repeat it.

You *definitely* heard that right.

In one second, your calm, comfortable mind is now in overdrive. A stunning mix of excitement and nerves sends you into a whirlwind of emotions. You hope your face is showing mostly excitement, but the camera doesn't lie. Either you passed the test and provided a wonderfully happy and candid moment, or your partner isn't going to post that particular reaction on social media.

But the truth is, you are excited . . . **and** nervous.

The journey of first-time fatherhood—throughout the nine months of pregnancy and the first year of your child's life—are among the most exciting, nerve-racking, exhausting, and remarkable days of your entire life. They are filled to the brim with new experiences, thoughts, questions, and daydreams—but often a lot of anxiety too.

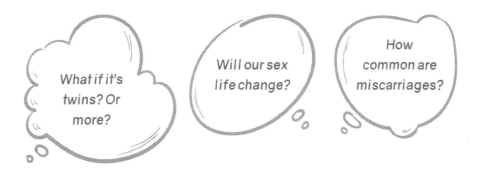

There is a lot of information out there for new dads—some of it more valuable than others—especially when considering the experience of dads in a post-COVID world. And in a modern age where dads are just as involved with the day-to-day duties as mothers, we go through our own series of anxieties, perspectives, and challenges. While a dad's experience may in some ways be similar to that of mothers, there are so many aspects of a father's journey that are remarkably different.

In our own experience, many of those unique dad perspectives throughout pregnancy and the first year are rarely, if ever, talked about and understood across wider society. That has been a huge motivation in writing this book and is among the most important things to remember at the outset—**this is a journey for you, too, as well as the mother of your child.**

As necessary as it is to look after your child's and partner's needs, you should never neglect your own mental health and wellness in the process. That's especially important because in whichever way you become a dad—whether you're married and have been trying for a while, or together and hadn't planned on it; whether the pregnancy is natural, accidental, a surrogacy, in vitro or something else entirely— we all face one simple truth: **we have to prepare.**

In this book, we're going to help you do just that. We'll do our best to answer all the questions that might be circling your brain as a dad-to-be. We'll go step-by-step through the first nine months of pregnancy and the first year of your child's life—answering everything we can along the way. We'll lay out important milestones to plan for, projects to prepare for, and offer reflections from our community of dads who have gone through it all, or our dads-to-be who are going through it now.

 # WHO ARE DADDILIFE BOOKS

DaddiLife Books is the publishing division of DaddiLife—the leading platform and community for modern-day dads. Formed 5 years ago with a mission to shine a light on the generational change of modern-day dads, the team has written about several topics, issues, and opportunities in the area and has grown to a community of over 150,000 dads.

Check us out at www.daddilife.com

Our goal with this book is to prepare you in the best way we possibly can. As a community of dads with a wide range of experience, we won't sugarcoat the process. And we promise to be honest about what you can expect. Often, we'll be relentlessly upbeat, but we'll be sure to tackle the difficult conversations too. Because whatever comes next, you can handle it. You can do this.

You're going to be a dad.

HOW TO USE THIS BOOK

This handbook is your go-to guide for everything you need to know during pregnancy and the first year of your baby's life. Within it, you'll find the practical science of fetal, neonatal, and infant development, as well as the experiences and milestones you and your partner should plan for. You'll gain insights from a whole community of dads through one-on-one interviews we've done with over fifty new dads and dads-to-be. These are dads from different countries, continents, cultures, and backgrounds, each of whom has lived through (or are living through) all stages of pregnancy and fatherhood in a pre- and post-COVID world.

We encourage you to read this book in any way you see fit.

If that happens to be chronologically in keeping with the pregnancy, that works. If it happens to be all at once in one very red-eyed and sleepless night, that works too. If you want to read ahead to know what to expect in the coming weeks or months, do what works for you.

Bookmark it, highlight pages and take notes. Take it with you camping, to work, on the subway or the train, to the doctor, the midwife, the doula, or the OB-GYN visits. Dirty it up a bit and really give these pages the once-over. Then the twice-over. And then the many times over.

This isn't intended to be a read once-and-forget-it kind of book because we've found that with first-time fatherhood, sometimes, things might not connect on the first pass. Then something might happen during pregnancy or that first year where suddenly the words

HOW THIS BOOK
IS ORGANIZED

This book has a few different parts in each chapter but let's start with something you most likely already know—a pregnancy, on average, lasts for forty weeks. Those forty weeks are divided into three trimesters. And let us save you some time at the outset when you cleverly point out that forty weeks seems equal to ten months, not nine months. While that is technically true, babies disregard Gregorian calendars. One week is seven days, four weeks is twenty-eight days, and aside from February, we know every month on our calendar has either thirty or thirty-one days.

In other words, your baby knows what a month should be better than your calendar. In other *other* words, your baby just helped teach the first lesson in pregnancy:

Time is relative.

Your baby is growing at their own pace, and although timelines such as the first, second, third trimester, and, ultimately, the delivery due dates can help you plan—for the most part, **your baby is calling the shots**.

So we're going to break each trimester down by the month. That means you can expect nine chapters to cover the pregnancy, three per trimester, and a few more chapters to cover the baby's first year of life. Further, we're going to break down each chapter of the pregnancy by the week. We won't do that post-birth because the forty weeks of pregnancy and their milestones are relatively consistent across the board—but once your baby arrives on the scene, they dance to the beat of their own drum and guidelines across the first few days, weeks and months, function much better than the more regimented structure of pregnancy.

In each chapter, you can expect five things:

A Monthly Overview – The big things to look forward to each month!

What's Happening with the Baby & Mother – The science and psychology of gestation and motherhood.

What's Happening with You – The highs and lows and everything in between that affect first-time dads.

Reflections from Our Dads – What other dads have experienced at this specific stage, taken from our interviews with 50 new dads and dads-to-be.

A Weekly Checklist – All the things you'll want to have ticked off the to-do list!

You'll also see these guys—our first-time dad medical team—who will be on hand throughout the book with terms to know and a few other helpful visuals to bring each section to life. Because each local area has slightly different medical professionals involved in gestation and childbirth (doctors, midwives, OB-GYNs, Doula's, etc.), we've simplified them to just 'doctors' in this book.

As an important disclaimer, the information we offer in this book is not intended or implied to be a substitute for professional medical advice, diagnosis, or treatment. Always seek out professional medical advice from your local doctor or other qualified healthcare providers regarding any questions you may have about specific medical conditions or treatment plans.

Beyond those standards, each chapter might have a few additional specifics that are unique to the month, as each phase of the journey brings its own surprises and milestones. And just like that, you've uncovered another lesson in pregnancy and fatherhood that's hard to teach:

Everything that happens next, happens in stages.

Even if you don't feel prepared right now for what comes next, you will be by the time that stage arrives. Because each stage is a small step, and every step is a lesson you'll take with you until you finally meet your beautiful baby—and beyond. You don't need to worry about buying a minivan or raising a toddler right now. You just need to focus on the stage you're in.

You just found out some incredible news, and you're about to embark on a brand-new journey. It's going to be a wonderful, fulfilling, and challenging journey. But this book is here to guide you, step-by-step, starting with day one.

PART ONE

THE FIRST TRIMESTER

The first trimester of pregnancy will cover the first thirteen weeks, or three months. During that time, your partner will go through a multitude of changes as the baby grows faster than flowers in the springtime.

By the time you confirm the pregnancy (often with a ridiculous amount of pregnancy tests), the baby is likely to be at least four weeks old already.

The starting point of the first trimester begins on the first day of your partner's last menstrual period (LMP). As a rule, that day is also what is used to calculate the estimated due date. However, this also means that by the time you find out about the baby, even with an extremely efficient five-day pregnancy test, the sperm meeting and fertilizing the egg is already old news.

But as we mentioned, your baby is growing at their own pace, and they're the one calling the shots—more on that later. For now, just know that the first trimester covers thirteen weeks, and for the first few of those, your baby is still keeping a pretty big secret: *the beginnings of life*.

CHAPTER ONE

MONTH ONE

The funny thing about the first month of pregnancy is that most of it happens "behind the scenes." The beginning of the month follows all the typical symptoms of your partner's menstrual cycle—only toward the end of the month might there be any noticeable changes.

At that point, your partner may experience some tenderness in and around their breasts, some nausea at certain points in the day, and maybe even cramping. But unless you were tracking and planning for a pregnancy down to the day, nothing will necessarily feel out of the ordinary . . .yet.

But behind the scenes, the first month lays the foundation for all the months to come.

THE START OF SOMETHING NEW

TERMS TO KNOW

Uterus – Also known as the womb, this is the focal point of the female reproductive system and the home for the baby throughout the pregnancy.

Menstruation – Also known as a period. This is a cycle where the woman's body releases blood and excess uterine lining through the vagina. Basically, it gets rid of the foundation of what could be a baby's home each month.

Endometrium – The mucus membrane lining of the uterus, which thickens during menstruation.

Oocyte – A cell in the ovary or immature egg which can turn into an ovum (mature egg).

Ovarian Follicles – Small, fluid-filled sac in the ovary that contains one immature egg or oocyte.

MOTHER AND BABY

The standard method of tracking pregnancy is to start with the first day of your partner's LMP. That means two things. One, the "first week" of the baby's development really has no baby at all. And two, we use the last period, not ovulation, to track pregnancy and determine due dates. Ovulation would technically be more accurate (when the egg is released to be fertilized), but it's also much harder to track in individual women.

For now, let's move forward by answering the age-old question: *What is a period?*

Every month, the female body prepares for a baby by lining the uterus with a thick mucus membrane called the endometrium. When an egg isn't fertilized, that excess tissue and blood are released from the body because there's no potential baby that needs the added cushion or protection.

This whole process is called menstruation.

Though specific cycle lengths differ, one thing's for sure: pre-menopausal women will menstruate or get their period every month. During that time, they'll experience a number of hormonal changes that cause cramps and bloating—likely some symptoms you've heard about before.

The period itself, however, is like a **reset button**.

It's completely natural, and it's also why a woman getting her period is often a telltale sign that they aren't pregnant. The reset button begins the next round of preparation for a new opportunity to reproduce.

YOU'RE GOING TO BE A DAD!

Toward the end of a woman's period, the ovaries are doing their best to prepare for the coming ovulation (the release of an egg, or sometimes more than one egg!). By the end of a period, one or two ovarian follicles (fluid sacs that hold the eggs) will have matured enough to release an immature egg, called an *oocyte*. But this oocyte isn't just any egg; this is the dominant egg. This egg has the strongest blood supply and produces more estrogen than any other. Remember, this process happens once a month, so, in other words, this egg = *Ovulee of the Month*.

You're welcome.

The egg will slide into the fallopian tube from the ovary, one of two tubes just outside the uterus, and await fertilization. Again, this entire process happens once a month. There's only one thing missing from this whole party getting started: you.

WHAT'S HAPPENING WITH YOU – PRE-CONCEPTION JITTERS

How are you feeling so far? This is the start, sure. However, it's also likely that you're not in the first week of pregnancy if you've picked up this book. In fact, you might be playing catch-up to get to the week you are now. But putting that aside for now, and no matter where you are in this process, try and take stock.

What's occupying your mind right now? Are you excited? Nervous? Upbeat?

There are no wrong answers — just observations.

What are you feeling the most? What thoughts do you keep circling back to?

For some, a positive pregnancy test can come as a surprise. For others, trying to get one can pose a real challenge. Whether you've been trying to get pregnant for days, months, or years, any negative result can be frustrating, disappointing, and dispiriting. Trying again and again can wear on anyone, and the longer it goes on, the more impactful those negative results can feel.

All said, it's a lot of build-up getting here, even if it's still the pregame. Before it all begins, and after it finally does, the barrage of questions can be more than prominent, and they can feel, quite simply, unending:

Will my baby be healthy? Do I have healthy sperm? Will the baby impact my relationship? Am I ready to take on this responsibility yet? Am I emotionally, psychologically, financially prepared for this change in my life? How will the impact of COVID-19 affect us?

All we can say right now is, take a breath. One, slow breath in. One, slow breath out. And then again. And again. Something we've discovered: no matter where we happen to be as expectant fathers in the pregnancy, we really come to lean on the power of information.

Your mind might already be constantly asking these questions because your brain is starting to funnel in a sort of instinct overdrive. Those instincts, at first, can come across as protective (even over-protective). They are concerned about your wellbeing, your future child's wellbeing, as well as that of the mother of your child. But, at their core, they're showing up to help mentally and physically prepare you.

To get you ready.

When you have gone through all the possibilities and can discern what things you can control and what you can't—that's often the only point where you can start to feel at ease. And more than anything, we want you to feel at ease. Even if easier said than done.

To do that, these sections will cover What's Happening with You. They'll not only give you information to help you prepare, but guidance on how to take care of yourself too. Also, to let you know that you're not alone in all this, we'll follow up these sections with reflections from other first-time dads and dads-to-be. They'll provide specific commentary on things discussed in the chapter, and include some of their own insights on how they've felt in certain moments, and how they've dealt with those issues.

And since there's no better time than the present, here's our first set of...

REFLECTIONS FROM OUR DADS

"It took us about 3 years to conceive with IVF. So getting to pregnancy was a massive high in the first place, especially as you only have 45 minutes to get your samples to the hospital!"

– Ben B. Norwich, UK

"I gotta tell you, it's not as easy to get pregnant as I thought. My wife was actually told she couldn't. We were planning, tracking ovulation, staying healthy, walking a lot, eating dates to 'soften the cervix'—and finally, against all odds, it happened."

– Cole F. North Carolina, US.

"If I could go back, I'd tell myself—relax, slow down, enjoy it. We thought it might be sooner, but the stress can stack up if you let it. Relax, slow down. Just enjoy it. Your baby is on the way when they're ready, and they're coming to you as fast as they can."

– Barrett E. Chicago, US.

THE MIRACLE OF CONCEPTION

TERMS TO KNOW

Egg – The female reproductive cell, also called an ovum or gamete.

Sperm – Spermatozoon, also known as spermatozoa, is the male reproductive cell. The tiny, white swimmers that look like little tadpoles.

Cervix – The lowest region of the uterus, and connects the uterus to the vagina through a narrow pathway.

Ovulation – The release of a mature egg from the female ovary that is able to be fertilized by a male spermatozoon.

Fallopian Tubes – Pair of tubes where the egg travels from the ovaries to the uterus.

MOTHER AND BABY

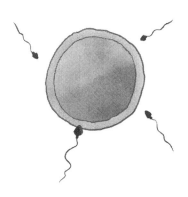

Last week we talked about the period, and started to talk about ovulation. Just as a refresher—the basic rundown of ovulation is when the ovaries release the dominant egg into one of two fallopian tubes. Once there, the egg awaits fertilization.

That's right, this week is where *you* enter the equation.

First, it should be noted that your baby is the combination of two very amazing cells. In fact, start thinking about the Olympics, NASCAR, Formula One, or drone racing—because not only is your baby made from a very competitive egg, but also a pretty speedy sperm.

Roughly 100 million sperm enter the vagina upon ejaculation and race down Cervix Road—a road which (for some reason, probably healthy evolution) has roadblocks in the form of cervical mucus. Only about 10% of sperm make it beyond the cervix because the cervical mucus works to filter out sperm that either don't move fast enough or have an abnormal shape (like two tails or a misshapen rather than oval head). Then, once inside the uterus, white blood cells also swarm the sperm, trying to remove the foreign body from . . . well, the body. Of the sperm that make it past the cervix, only about 1% of sperm will survive the onslaught of white blood cells.

All in all, only **1 in 14 million sperm** (roughly the same odds as winning the lottery!) will get through the defenses and enter the fallopian tube where the egg is waiting. However, there are also two tubes to choose from, but only one of them has an egg (or eggs), so this particular sperm doesn't only need to be fast but also good with directions. In other words, *winning the lottery has nothing on the miracle of life.*

Even with all of that behind them, the final threshold for the handful of surviving sperm is the egg itself. Your sperm went through a lot to get to this egg, and maybe a few other sperm are still swimming nearby. Conventional wisdom used to say that the fastest sperm is always the winner, but as it turns out, the sperm has to be *charming* too. The egg might reject some sperm that arrive first.

Even if this *whole* party was set up for the two to meet—a blind date, if you will—the egg is still waiting for the "right one."

So, what does all this mean?

Well, on the surface, it means *conception* can happen between days 12 and 16 of your partner's ovulation cycle, which means somewhere toward the end of Week 2 or the beginning of Week 3. But more than that, it means your baby is fast, smart and extremely charming! And if your sperm made it through the gauntlet and her egg accepted the offer, it's also a very lucky one. Whichever way you want to look at it, the day you find out your baby has been conceived, just keep in mind how lucky a day it is.

WHAT'S HAPPENING WITH YOU - NUTRITION & BREAKING THE HABITS

Every medical professional will constantly ask your partner throughout the pregnancy: *"How is your diet? How is your nutrition?"*

In the coming weeks (and throughout the pregnancy), your partner's cravings and food aversions can become extremely strong, so try to be conscious when they can only stomach certain things.

That being said, it's still important to know that everything your partner eats and drinks is going to be used by the baby during their development. If she drinks alcohol, smokes, or skips the prenatal vitamin because it smells like old fish (it happens), those choices can negatively impact the baby. But the bottom line, those are still *her choices to make*. We can't make them for her, **so what can we do?**

Well, we can try to make good choices too. And try to make them together.

If she chooses the salad with a light dressing, it probably won't help if you choose the greasy burger, fries, and a chocolate milk-shake all the time. If she shouldn't drink alcohol because it impacts the development of the baby's brain, is it a good idea for you to have a pint or two? If she can't smoke (not that it's ever a fantastic idea), are you going to keep lighting up around her? If she doesn't want to take her prenatal vitamin, will you do what you can to encourage her or make her feel bad for not doing so?

Solidarity, that's the name of the game.

When we find out that we have a baby on the way, the instinct is to suddenly change everything in a blink, but habits are hard to break. Very, **very** hard to break. We aren't recommending that you change every aspect of your life; we only want you to be conscious of your choices and honest with yourself.

If she's struggling, *how can you help?*

If you're struggling, *how can she help?* Or, perhaps more importantly, *what actions can you take to help yourself?*

Whether preconception or post, there's no better time than *right now* to jump on the healthier train. We know, most of us groan when we hear that. Sometimes it doesn't feel like there's enough time in the day to make those healthy choices. But try to keep in mind, the diet you've cultivated over your whole life, either good or bad, was for *you*.

Now, it's for more than just you.

I've got work. I forgot to grocery shop. Just a quick bite because I've got a busy day.

We're not going to lay out all the healthy options or try to guess any dietary restrictions—we know you probably know them. But during preconception, things like smoking and drinking in excess can slow down your swimmers or cut their count by millions, which can really harm the possibility of conceiving. Smoking has also been known to cause *ectopic pregnancy*, which is when the fertilized egg grows outside the woman's uterus, leading to a life-threatening condition for mother and baby. However, that also doesn't necessarily mean you should return to those good ol' habits after getting the positive result on the pregnancy test.

A baby is a lot to carry for anyone. Your partner might be physically holding your baby, and her nutrition will primarily impact the baby— but just remember—*you're a team*. In this, right now, your goal is to help each other.

If that starts with diet, it starts with diet.

If it's breaking the habits, then do what you feel you need to.

FOODS & DRINKS RECOMMENDED BY DOCTORS TO AVOID DURING PREGNANCY

High-Mercury Fish

Mercury is a highly toxic element and can be harmful to your partner's nervous system, immune system, and kidneys—as well as causing developmental problems for your baby. Not all fish are high in mercury, as it's often the result of pollutants in our seas, and larger fish can intake more of it, but some high-mercury fish to keep an eye out for include:

- Shark
- Swordfish
- Tuna (especially Bigeye Tuna)
- King Mackerel
- Marlin

Some doctors do still recommend fatty fish during pregnancy because they can be high in omega-3 fatty acids, which are very helpful for a growing baby. Those high omega-3, low mercury fish include:

- Salmon
- Anchovies
- Cod
- Flounder
- Haddock
- Tilapia

Undercooked or Raw Fish

Sorry, not many sushi options here. Raw fish, like shellfish, are often on the avoid list during pregnancy because they can be home to viral, bacteria-related or parasitic infections, such as the Norovirus, Vibrio, Salmonella, and Listeria.

Undercooked Meat

The rules of undercooked meat are similar to fish. Eating it can increase the risk of bacteria-related or parasitic infections, including Toxoplasma, E. coli, Listeria, and Salmonella. Bacteria like that can threaten the health of your growing baby, with some cases leading to stillbirth or neurological problems.

Even though Steak enthusiasts will be sad to hear it, the basic rule is that the safest way to consume all of those whole cuts of meat (sirloins, ribeye, filet) is to prepare them "well done" or make sure there's little-to-no pink when cut open. The same rules apply for cut meats (burgers, ground beef, minced pork). Those should always be cooked all the way through for safety.

Hot Dogs & Deli Meats

Hot dogs, ham, turkey, bologna, salami, and most anything quick-and-easy from the deli aisle have been placed in the avoid column because of the chemicals they're often steeped in before consumption. Some doctors make a small stipulation in this regard that these meats can be eaten only if steaming hot—hot enough to make those chemicals less prevalent and dangerous.

Either way, it still means cold-cut sandwiches are off the menu for now.

Raw Eggs

Like undercooked meats or fish, raw eggs can sometimes be contaminated with Salmonella, and pregnant women are often more susceptible to it. Salmonella can sometimes cause fever, nausea, vomiting, stomach cramps, and diarrhea. It has also, in rarer cases, been linked to contraction cramps that bring about premature labor.

Raw eggs can be found in:
- lightly scrambled eggs, poached eggs, or over-light/runny eggs
- some types of mayonnaise
- some types of salad dressings
- some types of ice creams

Too Much Caffeine

For most doctors, a couple of cups of coffee a day during pregnancy is okay. So long as the caffeine intake is lower than around 200 mg per day. Sometimes too much caffeine, or more than that amount, has been linked to restricting fetal growth and low birth weight.

Raw Sprouts

The basic rule of thumb is that raw things are off the menu. That also includes the plants from the ground like radishes, mung beans, clovers, and alfalfa sprouts as they, like many other raw food items, may be carrying Salmonella.

Unwashed Produce

Always get into the habit of washing produce before you eat it. In present and post- COVID-19 world, that's even more important. Unwashed produce can carry many of the bacteria already mentioned, but also be home to the Toxoplasma parasite.

Unpasteurized Foods & Drinks

Along with everything raw and undercooked, doctors also recommend avoiding anything unpasteurized. That can include milk, cheeses, and some fruit drinks, as they have been known to contain many harmful bacteria, including Listeria, Salmonella, E. coli, and Campylobacter.

Alcohol

Alcoholic beverages can cause a number of neurological and other problems during fetal development because it enters the bloodstream and affects them the same way as it does us—but then takes twice as long to leave their bloodstream. The lasting effects can be extremely dangerous to the baby as it has been linked to heart defects, facial deformities, and intellectual problems. More than that, it's been linked to many instances of miscarriage or stillbirth—so it's 100% best to avoid altogether.

REFLECTIONS FROM OUR DADS

"We had this huge build-up for months, and then a climactic downshift, even a depression because we weren't sure if we could have a kid. But man, when it happened—it was just, we couldn't believe it. A complete roller-coaster, and it was just getting started."
— Cole F.North Carolina, US.

"All I thought was, oh man, I really need to learn to cook! My menu is eggs, toast, and cereal . . . that's it."
— Kevin H. Utah, US.

"Don't let anybody trick you, tracking ovulation and 'getting lucky' at a structured time of day is not as exciting as it sounds. A bit of a relief when it finally happened, to be honest. My little guy needed a break!"
— James G.California, US

"We had an IVF pregnancy, and my partner had to take progesterone shots constantly in the beginning stages. That was definitely one of the lows of the whole pregnancy as she was in extreme pain. Progesterone is the hormone that tells the body - 'keep this thing alive' so it's super important for IVF pregnancies. It meant a big needle, every 3rd day, which were so extreme that they actually caused long term skin damage - on top of the oral progesterone too."
- Field C. Seattle, US.

☑ WEEKLY CHECKLIST

☐ Possible sexy-time for your partner's optimal ovulation!

☐ Think about getting a nutrition journal or tracker (if you're the planning type).

☐ Try out some healthier lifestyle changes:
  ☐ Grocery shop together.
  ☐ Find some fun meals to cook (even some desserts).
  ☐ Take a walk together.
  ☐ See if there's an exercise plan out there that you'd like to try—and a pregnancy-safe one for your partner.

WEEK 3

CREATING DNA

TERMS TO KNOW

Zygote – A fertilized egg that includes a combination of male and female gametes. Sperm + Egg = Zygote.

Blastocyst – A big cluster of cells that come from the zygote multiplying. Zygote x Itself = Blastocyst.

Chromosomes – Part of the cell that carries genetic information in the form of genes – DNA!

Human Chorionic Gonadotropin (hCG) – The pregnancy hormone! Helps prepare a woman for developing a baby and causes a number of changes to her body.

Progesterone – The other pregnancy hormone! The steroid hormone that prepares the uterus for the egg and maintains the pregnancy throughout.

Estrogen – Primary female sex hormone that helps develop and maintain the reproductive system and secondary sex characteristics.

MOTHER AND BABY

As you know now from earlier, conception likely happened at the end of Week 2 or at the beginning of Week 3. To further define conception: if the egg accepts the sperm, and the sperm is able to fertilize it, then they become a team—a zygote. And that *zygote* will eventually become your baby!

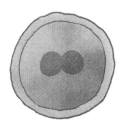

You and your partner's DNA come together, and the chromosomes combine to create your baby's unique genetic code. In those early days, very likely Week 3, the baby's sex and genetic features will all be determined.

After that, all that's left is to grow, baby, grow!

Within twenty-four hours of conception, the zygote starts dividing into multiple cells and travels down the fallopian tube. By the end of week 3, the zygote has multiplied enough to become a *blastocyst* (just as cool as it sounds).

The blastocyst divides itself into layers; the inner layer will become the fetus (the baby), and the outer will become the *placenta*— the life supply of the baby throughout gestation. To make it all happen, the blastocyst implants itself into the endometrium (the wall of the uterus) and starts to produce the pregnancy hormone, *human chorionic gonadotropin* (hCG), which is the substance that's detected by pregnancy tests.

And after all this has happened on the inside, it's also where things start changing for your partner on the outside. All the symptoms she had before were more likely traditional menstrual symptoms, but this production of hCG and other hormones brings about pains and changes that go above and beyond typical menstrual symptoms.

These are known as **early pregnancy symptoms**.

More hormone production in her body, like estrogen and progesterone, will likely mean more nausea and quite a few other symptoms that we'll get into in the following few chapters. At the same time, it's worth knowing that pregnancy will pause your partner's menstrual cycle for at least the next nine months, and in some cases, for months after your baby is born (especially if your partner is breastfeeding). For most women, that's one of the few "perks" of the whole endeavor!

If this all sounds extensive, it's only to emphasize a very important point: *creating life really is a miracle*. The number of things that need to go right for all of those steps to work is nothing short of remarkable. So, before you move forward in experiencing the continued mind-blowing marvel of pregnancy and birth, it's great to just take into account the true miracle of conception.

Simply being here, it really is *amazing*.

WHAT'S HAPPENING WITH YOU – EARLY PREGNANCY SYMPTOMS & YOU

Over the course of the pregnancy, your partner might encounter any of a very long list of pregnancy symptoms. Each woman will experience these differently, and some months will be better than others—but without a doubt, their body is changing, and they are going to feel it in a number of different ways.

In the beginning, early pregnancy symptoms are easily confused with typical period symptoms. However, there are a few tell-tale symptoms that can be a good indicator of conception—and a precursor of symptoms to come.

Breast Changes

Often one of the first things women will experience are changes to their breasts. Their nipples might darken, along with their areolas (the colored circles around the nipple). Their breasts might become sore as their mammary glands start the transition to making milk. Later on, their nipples might even get chapped.

What can you do?

Invest in some nipple butter as an early gift. This helps prevent dry skin and can be soothing, possibly even . . . *stimulating*. Still, be gentle...

Nausea & Morning Sickness

When the pregnancy hormone (hCG) starts moving through your partner's body, it brings with it some pretty intense nausea and even

53

REFLECTIONS FROM OUR DADS

"It's a little crazy, my wife loved onions. She would have them on literally everything—fried, diced, whole, onion rings. As soon as she became pregnant, they became her least favorite food just because of the smell."
- David R. North Carolina, US.

"When it came to morning sickness or just nausea in general: ginger candies, sour candies (even Sour Patch Kids), and diffusing peppermint oil all seemed to help."
— Richard T. New Hampshire, US.

"I thought of the 9 months as a way to psychologically get myself in *that* place"
— Cole F. North Carolina, US.

"They call it morning sickness but my wife experienced it at any and all points of the day during the first trimester. It's difficult because you're not sure what you can do to lessen it as so many medications aren't allowed for pregnant women. But luckily, our doctor was able to prescribe a safe anti-nausea which really seemed to help."
— Dean F. Kansas, US.

☑ WEEKLY CHECKLIST

☐ Focus on hydration (about a half-gallon/ 2 L per day!)

☐ Get a pregnancy journal to prepare to write everything down

   ☐ It doesn't have to be anything fancy; it could even be the notepad on your phone, but it's great to be able to look back on key moments.

   ☐ Another more modern option is documenting your Social Media stories and saving those big updates—watching the collage of moments at the end is extremely rewarding!

WEEK 4

OF IMPLANTATIONS & EMBRYOS

TERMS TO KNOW

Embryo – Name of baby up to seven weeks—when it turns into a collection of cells!

Amnion – The thing that forms a fluid-filled cavity (the amniotic sac) and surrounds the baby embryo like a protective shield!

Placenta – The organ that connects the baby to the uterus of the mother, eventually the main life supply for the baby; helping with nutrition, breathing, and relieving the . . . excretions.

OB-GYN – A medical specialization in obstetrics (pregnancy, childbirth, postpartum) and gynecology (health of female reproductive system).

Local Doctor/Midwife - Trained health professional that helps during labor, delivery, and after the birth.

Doula– Someone who can provide emotional and physical support throughout pregnancy (often doesn't have formal medical training).

MOTHER AND BABY

Last we saw the blastocyst (still cool), they
were separating into layers within the uterus.
So, what changes happen in Week 4 that gets
everything really going?

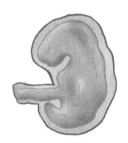

The answer: *embryo*.

Your baby is now an embryo—roughly the size
of a poppyseed!

Let's look at this process in detail: The fertilized egg (zygote) first
divided into the ball of cells (blastocyst), which then implanted
itself into the lining of the uterus (endometrium) through a process
called *implantation*. So much vocabulary! Anyway, about half of
that microscopic ball of cells begins to form into the embryo (which
already has the blueprints for all your baby's future organs!), while
the other half starts to form the placenta and *amniotic sac* (basically
a bacta chamber from *Star Wars*).

To get even more specific, the embryo is actually divided into three
layers:

Ectoderm– The outer layer that develops into the nervous system,
eyes, skin, and hair.

Mesoderm– The middle layer that develops into the baby's heart,
kidneys, bones, muscles, and reproductive organs.

Endoderm– The inner layer that develops into the lungs, liver, and
digestive system.

But all that is happening with the baby embryo—*so what's happening with your partner?*

Well, if your partner wasn't feeling those early symptoms last week, some of them will likely show up this week. In addition to the few we mentioned, like nausea (morning sickness) and sore breasts, she might also be feeling a good bit of bloating this week from that uptick of progesterone in her system. Compound that with some cramping, likely from implantation, and it's not a very fun combo.

She might also feel some very intense fatigue this week—growing a baby is hard work, and that little embryo is already giving her a run for her money. To add to that, she might be experiencing the beginnings of some mood swings caused by those rapidly fluctuating pregnancy hormones—or, another name for it, "hormones-on-a-rampage."

All said, the best thing you can do this week is listen to your partner's body. She might be craving a nap, and if there's time, encourage her to take it. Hey, you could probably use a little siesta too! It's been an eventful month already.

Because by Week 4, whether you both have found out or not, the baby is definitely on board.

WHAT'S HAPPENING WITH YOU - SCHEDULING YOUR FIRST DOCTOR VISIT

We're going to go ahead and assume you *did* find out this week. We'll also assume you had some sort of frantic race to the store where you picked out every pregnancy test you could find and the biggest bottle of water to boot.

Of course, we don't all find out by Week 4, but if we do...

We've got to confirm.

So that's the very next step. Once you get that positive result on the pregnancy test, or once you get enough symptoms that pregnancy seems *more than likely*, it's time to call the doctor. Typically, the 'doctors' you're looking for (especially at first) will be from an obstetrician & gynecology office if you're in the US and Canada (also known as an OB-GYN). If you're in the UK or Australia (or most anywhere else), it's likely your local GP or midwife who will help you book your first appointment. For simplicity, whoever they are, we just want to remind you that we'll refer to them as 'doctors' from here on in.

Just so you're aware, the doctors might want to wait until the eight-week mark when the embryo has developed into a fetus to schedule a visit, but if you ask, they can often accommodate an appointment sooner. However, six to eight weeks is a common range for when they'll want to schedule that first appointment.

A common name for this appointment is the *First Prenatal Ultrasound*.

The ultrasound, as the name implies, is when the doctors use some really intense soundwaves, almost like sonar, to detect and visualize your baby's movements. You won't necessarily get an ultrasound during every visit over the course of the pregnancy, but they are definitely some of the most exciting visits because they're where you finally get to see your baby!

All that said, this first visit is also your chance to start *choosing* your doctors. Don't feel pressured that the very first doctor's office you go to is who you're stuck with for the duration—it's very common to try out different places until you find the right fit for both you and your partner. And in some cases, you'll get seen by different doctors throughout the pregnancy.

There are a lot of things to consider when choosing a doctor: location from your home, cost, and how well you get along. After all, you will be seeing these people a lot! Under typical circumstances, you can expect the following visits during the pregnancy:

Weeks 4-28:	Weeks 28-36:	Weeks 36-40:
(first and second trimester)	(third trimester)	(third trimester)
1 prenatal visit per month	1 prenatal visit every 2 weeks	1 prenatal visit every week

That comes out to about a total of 12 visits over the course of the pregnancy and that's common in the US and Canada. For many other places like the UK, 10 is usually the golden number of visits spread out over those nine months.

Something else you can start thinking about this week, and discussing with your partner, are the various ways in which babies can be born. It may seem a little overwhelming at first, but there are actually a lot of options:

- Vaginal Birth
- Natural Birth
- Scheduled Cesarean Section
- Unplanned Cesarean Section
- Vaginal Birth After C-Section (VBAC)
- Scheduled Induction

What's more, COVID-19 also resulted in a shift as to **where** many parents have decided to have their baby. Less access to hospitals meant a lesser feeling of safety as infections were more widespread. There have also been more intense restrictions with mothers having to wear masks, babies without the ability to have skin-to-skin contact after birth, and a cut-off of fathers being "in the room" - all of which had many parents seeking alternatives.

There has been a huge uptick in interest for births to be done at home with a midwife or in specified birthing centers for instance, rather than hospitals.

Although we're not making recommendations ourselves on where or how you should elect to have your baby, this is a great time to start assessing all your options. What you might discover in talking with your partner or your provider are strong feelings on the matter that you had no way of knowing about before this decision was suddenly upon you. With that, we encourage you to research each option as much as you can, and talk as much as you can with your partner. Even if you both had expectations ahead of time, that could still change.

Be open, be adaptive, and find what works best for both of you.

REFLECTIONS FROM OUR DADS

"The way I found out was that I came home from work, my wife was making some food, she asked for a spoon—which I thought was weird—then I went there, and a pregnancy test was in the drawer. Positive. She was waiting, and we both just started laughing."
— Cole F.North Carolina, US.

"When I found out I was genuinely in shock! Particularly as she announced it in such a funny way I was almost positive it was a joke at first!"
- Amish P. St Albans, UK.

"I was speechless. I was overwhelmed. I had a life goal to become a dad since I was very young, but to actually hear it, was something else. Because of how I've grown up and how I grew up with my dad I knew it would be okay, and it was definitely exciting but also totally overwhelming."
- Ziko T, Surrey, UK

"She called me upstairs, the phone was recording but I didn't see it, and she says she's pregnant. We weren't planning for a baby at all. A million thoughts start rushing but I just smiled and hugged her, because I knew she was nervous. It wasn't immediate excitement for us—but eventually it washed over us, and we couldn't be happier."
— Taylor W. Washington, US.

☑ WEEKLY CHECKLIST

☐ Get an at-home pregnancy test! (Or a few of them).

☐ Schedule your first doctor's appointment: *the eight-week ultrasound!*
  ☐ It's also possible they'll help you confirm the pregnancy earlier than that.

☐ As an extra challenge, try and determine your own due date!
  ☐ 40 weeks from the first day of your partner's LMP.

CHAPTER TWO

MONTH TWO

It's official, *your partner is pregnant!* Although you may not be seeing the many changes happening with your baby beneath the surface, your partner is definitely starting to feel them. During the second month, those early pregnancy symptoms like morning sickness, heartburn, breast tenderness, excessive urination, and fatigue might all come into play. Creating a baby takes an enormous toll on the body—and your baby is going through numerous changes to prove it. Over the course of the month, your baby will develop a face, hands, feet, and even a heart, leading to one of the most incredible moments of the entire pregnancy—*the first time you hear their heartbeat.*

More than the physical discomforts of early pregnancy symptoms, there will also be a lot of overlapping thoughts or concerns from your partner. Some concerns you'll share, and some might be unique to either you or to her. The best way to deal with them is to have an open dialogue from the very beginning. It can be a real relief to know when you're both *nervous*—and *excitement* is that much better when it can be shared.

This month, you may also be surprised by your first bout of **sympathy pains.** As strange as it sounds, a lot of first-time dads experience them—and so do many veteran dads! For a long time, these sorts of feelings in dads used to be dismissed as "psychosomatic" responses or placebo effects, but new research actually helps prove that there are fundamental hormonal and physiological changes that can happen within a dad's body and brain in these first months, throughout pregnancy, and after the child is born. The precise reasons for it we'll get into later in this section, but don't be surprised if you start to feel some of the common discomforts that your partner feels during this first month. We might have nausea, an increased or decreased appetite, or even really severe fatigue.

Just remember, whatever happens next: *you're a team.*

You and your partner will be each other's support, and staying involved in the process is the best way of maintaining a positive mental attitude for you both. You are connected in this journey, and you're taking it together.

WEEK 5

NEURAL TUBE, ROLL OUT!

TERMS TO KNOW

Morning Sickness - Up to 80% of pregnant women experience first-trimester nausea and vomiting. That queasy, sick-to-your stomach feeling may be dubbed "morning sickness," but for many, it's really "all-day sickness" since it can hit at any time of day, including in the middle of the night.

Neural Tube – In an embryo, the hollow structure from which the brain and spinal cord form.

Central Nervous System – The system that controls everything we do—breathing, walking, thinking, and feeling. It's made up of the brain, spinal cord, and a lot of nerves.

MOTHER AND BABY

This week, your baby is about the size of a sesame seed at .13 inches! The fifth week kicks off the second month of the first trimester, and it's also the first time your baby will look less like a collection of cells and more like a tadpole. (complete with a tail!) Still, this also might be the first time you're finding out about your partner being pregnant if they've only missed their period the week before!

In any case, this week, the embryo is still extremely small. Its three layers of the ectoderm (outer layer and nervous system), mesoderm (middle layer and reproductive system), and endoderm (inner layer and digestive system) are starting to take shape. That said, the big player this week is the ectoderm. One of the first things to develop is the baby's *nervous system*, and to do this, the baby embryo gets to work on making a whole collection of nerves and then promptly rolling them up (like a newspaper to whack a fly) into a tube called the *neural tube*.

This is also what gives the embryo its tadpole appearance, as the neural tube predominantly finds its shape from the spinal cord giving that natural curve and the brain creating the bulge at the top. This early developmental stage is crucial, and one of the most vital nutrients for neural tube development is folate (or folic acid). A majority of prenatal vitamins will have it, but it's best to double-check and make sure your partner is getting a sufficient amount.

However, this also brings us back to how your partner is feeling.

Right now, she may well be feeling some of those early pregnancy symptoms. Morning sickness can really start to crank up this week, and again, "morning" isn't entirely accurate because the nausea and discomfort can show up at *any* time of day. If it's starting to get more pronounced, look into acupressure wristbands or look for a prenatal supplement with lots of Vitamin B6. Both really seem to help, especially early on.

Your partner might also feel completely exhausted this week, with extra cravings for naps or relaxation time on the couch. There's really not much she can do about that other than listen to her body, or perhaps get some intermittent physical activity like a walk or light exercise.

Another big change this week can be the sudden urge to pee—a lot. Her kidneys are expanding as part of the process, and as a Catch-22, doctors will also encourage her to drink *more* water. If you're out and about, be sure to think ahead so that she has easy access to a bathroom.

All said, whether she is feeling all, some, or none of these early symptoms, it isn't any reason to sound the alarm. Women experience pregnancy differently, and some will experience different symptoms at different times. What might be more important to observe is how the news of pregnancy has impacted *her.*

Is she excited? Distant? Has she expressed any worries or feelings of elation?

Where does she stand right now?

At this point, the important thing to keep in mind is your awareness of the situation, rather than anything actionable. Just observe, ask your own questions, and do what you feel will help both you and your partner. It's still early, and you're both doing great!

WHAT'S HAPPENING WITH YOU - THE FEAR OF MISCARRIAGES

One of the biggest fears of any pregnancy is the possibility of a *miscarriage*—an event that results in the loss of the fetus before twenty weeks of pregnancy. As it goes, miscarriages can happen for any number of medical reasons, and a majority of those reasons aren't within anyone's control.

The most common miscarriages occur before a woman even knows they're pregnant, which makes gauging their frequency pretty tough to do. Some doctors estimate as many as half of pregnancies can end in miscarriage, but most agree the range is closer to 10-20%. This statistic isn't here to scare you, but to help make you aware that miscarriages are more common than they're made out to be.

The reason they're not talked about is because they can be really difficult to talk about. The longer you and your partner know about the baby, the harder the miscarriage can be to cope with. At the same time, the longer the baby spends developing, the less and less likely a miscarriage will be. Although miscarriages can occur in 10% of women in the first trimester, they drop steadily to 5% by the second trimester, and continue to drop off from there.

The best advice is to talk to your doctors about the risks of pregnancy with you and your partner—and what you can do to lessen the potential for a miscarriage. If you've experienced a miscarriage in the past, take time to talk to your partner and make sure you both feel physically and emotionally ready to start trying again. There's no timeline for this process. When you're ready, you're ready. But just know that having a miscarriage doesn't mean you can't have a baby— as many as 87% of women who experienced a miscarriage went on to carry a baby full-term.

REFLECTIONS FROM OUR DADS

"My wife is Type-1 Diabetic and was told that she'd never have a baby. Compound that with some of my own kidney problems and we went into the whole situation a little more on alert. We did experience miscarriages, three if I'm being honest, and every one hurt in their own way. But now, all these years later, we have three healthy, beautiful children—and we couldn't be happier. It's a full house!"
— Noah A. Texas, US

"My initial reaction was 'lets get the nursery ready.' I'm talking like day 1 of week 1 finding out! But looking back, I rushed into setting up the bed etc, and didn't need to do that straight away. Our baby sleeps in our room for the first few months and I had to have an adjustment of how things work."
- Jon P. London, UK.

"My focus was immediately on the practical stuff. What do we need to buy? What lists should we start to make? When do I need to start thinking about classes?"
- Amish P. St Albans, UK.

☑ WEEKLY CHECKLIST

☐ Get a jump start on how, depending on
where you live, your insurance might cover
pregnancy and birth before your first prenatal
appointment to wrap your head around costs
and probe for the right questions once you get there.

☐ Think of any other questions you'd like to ask the doctors:

 ☐ *Can we travel?*

 ☐ *Is it safe to exercise? For how long?*

 ☐ *Are there any medications we should avoid?*

 ☐ *Are there any foods or diet plans you recommend?*

 ☐ *When should we book our next appointment?*

 ☐ *If we have additional questions, who can we contact?*

BABY GOT FACE

TERMS TO KNOW

Circulatory System – Also known as the cardiovascular system, it moves blood throughout the body, including the veins that carry blood to the heart and arteries that carry blood away from it.

Pituitary Gland – Gland found at the base of the brain, controls the growth and development of other endocrine glands.

Toxoplasmosis – Disease dangerous to unborn children, often transmitted through undercooked meat, soil, or cat feces—make sure you change the kitty litter!

MOTHER AND BABY

Little lentil bean (.25 inches)! By Week 6, the baby has already doubled in size from the previous week, and they're about to double again next week. What's most exciting about Week 6 is simply how much  is happening with them. During this time, your baby is developing a face complete with a jaw, chin, cheeks, optic nerves for future eyes, and little dimples for future ears. They can't see or hear anything just yet, and they still look more tadpole than human, but the foundation of what's happening is simply amazing!

Another huge part of Week 6 is the heart transforming from a simple tube to the complete four-chambered organ we all know and love. In fact, the heart alone is the size of your baby a couple weeks ago (a poppy seed) and is already beating at a steady pace of 105-110 bpm. This means is that in addition to the nervous system, the baby's circulatory system is getting its first test drive.

Week 6 also sees the start of development on the lungs, kidneys, pituitary gland (master gland in charge of hormones), intestines, and liver. If that wasn't enough, the embryo, now covered in a fine layer of translucent skin, is growing limbs. But these early limbs don't look like much just yet. Right now, they look a lot more like little fish-fins. But over the next few weeks, with some significant growth, they will stretch out into little arms and legs, and split off further at their ends to develop fingers and toes.

The last thing to mention about Week 6 is what's becoming of the neural tube. As we mentioned, it's already taking shape into the brain and spinal cord—but it's also starting to close. The neural tube closing forges the way for communication between the brain and the spine. At the end of nine weeks, it'll be completely closed.

With all that going on, it's likely your partner is feeling some pretty intense changes herself. Her fatigue might be worsening, and her breasts may be increasingly sore (and also getting bigger). The extreme need to pee can kick up too, even from last week. As hCG (the main pregnancy hormone) continues to direct more blood flow to the pelvic region, the urge to pee goes up at the same time (or the *feeling* that she needs to pee).

Additionally, with an almost definite rise in progesterone this week, your partner might also experience some pretty intense gas and bloating. Your doctors may recommend lots of water and fiber-rich foods like oatmeal, soybeans, chia seeds, avocados, sweet potatoes, and (conveniently enough for this week) lentils, to avoid constipation. But it's also nice to live by the *better out than in* policy on long car rides.

Crack a window, laugh, and make some funny memories!

WHAT'S HAPPENING WITH YOU - EMOTIONAL ROLLER-COASTERS

We've covered quite a few of the early pregnancy symptoms, but something we haven't discussed in detail is the effect of pregnancy hormones on your partner's mood. The drastic increase in estrogen, progesterone, and hCG streaming through your partner's body is a lot like taking a cup of soda at the machine and then dragging it across every nozzle to get a sampling of each flavor.

Her body has become a rich mixture of chemicals, and it's still working really hard to sort itself out. While it's doing so, it's anybody's guess as to what flavor of emotion will dominate that cup of soda. On any given day, she might experience anxieties about the pregnancy, difficulties with her changing body, and general life hardships. As those hormones are preparing her body and the developing baby for the upcoming birth in a plethora of different ways, her emotions and reactions can be dialed up to 11.

And, in a lot of ways, **she might not feel like she has control over them.**

The slightest inconvenience might bring her to tears, and the smallest relief might make her elated with joy. Even some women who didn't consider themselves to be particularly emotional before pregnancy might suddenly feel overwhelmed by a touching movie scene or relentlessly angry at everyday traffic. Not all women will experience pregnancy hormones the same, but every woman *will* have that influx of hormones in their body. Estrogen production alone in those first twelve weeks increases 10,000%!

As far as how to help your partner cope with these hormones, it'll depend on the situation. Sometimes your partner might want to be alone, or cry it out, or have you close by for comfort. The best advice we can give is to take it as it comes, be supportive, and try not to take these fluctuations personally—even if you might be taking the brunt of these mood swings. They often don't have a lot to do with you to begin with.

As we know, letting comments slide or roll off our shoulders isn't always as easy as it sounds. But as much as we want to be the perfect helper for our partner, those anxieties and everyday challenges can weigh on us too.

If you're finding it hard to maintain enthusiasm, or act how you feel you're *supposed* to, it might be a good time to reach out to a friend, a parent, a third-party, or even a therapist. Emotions during pregnancy can be overwhelming for both you and your partner, so it's a good idea to reflect on how you're feeling as openly and honestly as you can.

REFLECTIONS FROM OUR DADS

"I actually talked with my father early on, after finding out about pregnancy. To end the suspense, our first child was a happy accident, and I was unsure about being a father, even a bit shaken up at the time. But my own father helped me. He said, *If I could have my time back, the only change I'd make would be to have kids even sooner. You'll feel the same someday.* It was massively comforting to hear. And he was right."

– Alex M. London, UK

"I didn't believe pregnancy hormones were a big deal at first. But then my partner, who almost never overreacts or gets overly emotional, started crying after a minor little dispute on price while shopping. I was surprised, followed her out to help—she physically couldn't stop crying! But an hour later we were laughing about it."

— Emmanuel V. Texas, US.

"There was definitely tension in the early days of pregnancy around what type of birth we were going to have. I wanted a hospital birth so that all the safety measures were covered, whereas my wife wanted a birthing center. When we talked it through I realized that a lot of that came from my most recent experience of childbirth where my sister lost 4 pints of blood in giving birth so I felt the need to be ultra-safe."

– Damian C. Tonbridge, UK.

☑ WEEKLY CHECKLIST

☐ Start practicing how to prepare meals hygienically (after COVID we all know what that means, a good bit of handwashing).

☐ Wear gloves when emptying cat litter or gardening to minimize the risk of *toxoplasmosis*, a disease that can come from cat feces, soil, or undercooked meat.

 ☐ If you have a cat, go ahead and take care of changing the kitty litter for your partner whenever possible.

☐ Schedule a dental check-up as soon as you can; issues like gum disease can harm the developing baby, so it's great to get a jump on it—and you get a fresh, clean smile out of the deal!

7

THE CROWN-RUMP

Umbilical Cord – The narrow cord of tissue that connects the baby with the placenta.

Leukorrhea – Discharge from the vagina that may occur during pregnancy—no need to worry when it's thin, white, and pretty much odorless.

"Crown to Rump" – Ultrasound measurement from the "crown" of the baby's head to the bottom of their buttocks (rump).

Mucus Plug – Collection of mucus in the cervix to protect the baby from many different bacteria.

MOTHER AND BABY

Baby Blueberry (.51 inches)! As the title of Week 7 suggests, the baby has once again doubled in size and is now 1 cm in length from "crown to rump" (or the top of their head to the bottom of their buttocks), which is the traditional measure that doctors use in an ultrasound to determine your baby's development.

In Week 7, the baby's brain is on a growth binge, far outpacing the rest of their body. It's also the reason why the forehead pushes farther forward than the rest of the face, giving the new fetus a somewhat lopsided appearance. And speaking of the face, your baby is now developing eyelids to cover those optical nerves, inner ears to help with balance, and nostrils on their little mound of a nose.

However, some of the faster developments this week are the limbs, which are growing cartilage for the starting point of arm and leg bones. Those little budding limbs are also stretching out and preparing to flatten at the edges to form feet and hands.

Finally, the umbilical cord is really taking shape this week. This little tube is the lifeline between the baby and your partner, moving much-needed nutrients and blood to the baby and carrying away any waste.

Speaking of your partner, Week 7 has them going through a number of changes too. The first is within the cervix. As a result of all these hormonal changes, the cervix begins protecting the uterus from bacteria by producing a milky white substance called *leukorrhea*. This substance gathers to form a **mucus plug** that shields the baby from bacteria—but it also means that your partner might experience some odorless discharge.

Beyond that, Week 7 also marks the start of the "pregnancy glow." However, like a lot of conventional talk about pregnancy, this phenomenon should be taken with a grain of salt. While some women experience the "glow" of pregnancy, it's actually a result of increased blood flow to the face (and throughout the body to accommodate for growing baby.) That said, while some women may feel the glow, others might experience an over-production of oil on the skin that can lead to acne.

Regardless of whether your partner sees themselves as "glowing" or feeling in need of a new skincare routine, you can help them to find solace in the fact that they also developed their now-refined pregnancy superpower: *superhuman smell.*

Go ahead, test it out this week.

Like all great power, it comes with great responsibility. Some favorite foods might taste *way* better, but just a whiff of others might cause more morning sickness. In that way, your partner might also be experiencing their first pregnancy cravings. There's no real way to guess what your partner might crave, or what time of day they might crave it—but it's likely to be a strong craving. Some infamous ones are fried pickles at two in the morning, or a nice bowl of ice cream right after breakfast. There's really no guessing, but it's pretty fun to find out!

WHAT'S HAPPENING WITH YOU - WHEN TO SHARE THE NEWS?

Perhaps you've already had your very first prenatal appointment, or maybe it's still coming up next week. Either way, the pregnancy is probably feeling a bit more real by the day. Your baby and your partner have likely been occupying your thoughts for the past few weeks, and when that happens, it almost feels *impossible* not to share that news with someone.

That someone might be a parent, a best friend, or a sibling, as it's likely the first person you hope to tell is someone close to you. When it comes down to it, there are no set-in-stone rules as far as when to tell people about pregnancy. However, there is a pretty big difference between telling people close to you about pregnancy and *announcing* your pregnancy to the world. Announcements we'll get to later—but for now, this is just sharing the news to those who are closest to you.

Again, we can't tell you exactly when the right time is, but a common time for first-time dads to share the news is after confirmation from the first prenatal ultrasound. In a lot of ways, that first visit will confirm the baby for you as well. However, there's nothing wrong with telling people close to you as soon as you get the positive pregnancy test, but it's also important to be mindful of the first-trimester miscarriage statistics.

Whenever you decide, telling people you love about your exciting news can be a fantastic moment, and it can even make you feel closer to them. Whenever you feel the time is right, or when you're just too excited to keep it in any longer—*share the wonderful news!*

REFLECTIONS FROM OUR DADS

"I definitely became wary of people sharing the news on social media without me and my partner having a chance to first—but it was actually really amazing to see the look on my parents' faces when we told them over Facetime. It was during COVID, so we couldn't see them in person just yet, but we screen-recorded the call to keep as a great memory!"
— David R. North Carolina, US.

"I gotta say, midnight trips to Taco Bell for a Cheesy Gordita Crunch really drove home that the pregnancy was, indeed, *real*. And delicious."
— Kevin H. Utah, US.

"My wife's friend had the superhuman smell so bad that her husband couldn't even open the fridge while she was inside the house!"
- Keith G. , U.S.

"A word of warning to the dads to be doing DIY in early stage pregnancy – we were doing the new bathroom in that early stage, and unfortunately my partner now associates the brand new bathroom with being ill! In particular, when we put the new toilets in with the sealants – that smell of sealant is now a reminder of that part of her life."
- Louis M. Surrey, UK.

☑ WEEKLY CHECKLIST

☐ Get prepared to help battle morning sickness with a quick trip to the pharmacy:
- ☐ Ginger or lemon drops.
- ☐ Saltine crackers.
- ☐ Mints.
- ☐ Lemonade.
- ☐ Ginger Ale.
- ☐ Gatorade/Powerade.

☐ Do some *aversion tests:*
- ☐ What is causing morning sickness if it has already arrived?
- ☐ You might start noticing a change in your partner's desires for a few favorite foods (even possibly the smell of your deodorant).

☐ Think about telling close friends & family the wonderful news!

HELLO LOVELY HEARTBEAT

TERMS TO KNOW

Gestational Sac – Fluid-filled structure surrounding the embryo during the first few weeks of development.

Amniotic Sac – Fluid-filled structure surrounding and protecting the fetus until birth.

Digestive System – System of organs used to break down food, extract nutrients, and excrete waste.

MOTHER AND BABY

Week 8 is arguably the first week where your baby really starts looking like a *baby*. The cute little tail of the spinal cord isn't gone yet, but the limbs have stretched out and flattened, the head has found its

shape, and you can see the torso with a little belly that connects everything together. To think that all of this happened in just two months is nothing short of amazing.

In Week 8, the baby is roughly the size of a kidney bean (.63 inches and .04 ounces)!

They are starting to develop reproductive organs at this stage of development as their genitals are becoming testes or ovaries. Neither of those reproductive organs will show up on an ultrasound yet, but they are definitely starting to develop. The baby's digestive system is also being formed, even though there isn't actually enough room for it in that little belly. For now, most of the intestines have relocated to the umbilical cord until the baby has enough room in their abdomen to support them. All that said, the embryo is still getting all its nourishment from the gestational sac (remember that *Star Wars* bacta chamber?) as the placenta is still forming. However, the gestational sac is also one of the things that shows up first in the prenatal ultrasound.

That's right, if you haven't met up with your doctors already, you'll probably go to the big event this week—the one where both you and your partner not only confirm the pregnancy (if you haven't already) but experience your first ultrasound!

Although the changes for your partner on the inside are relatively similar to previous weeks, the psychological impact of that first ultrasound is powerful. In fact, that compounded with all the other thoughts from these last few weeks, it might just trigger her first batch of extremely vivid pregnancy dreams—more on that later.

WHAT'S HAPPENING WITH YOU - THE FIRST HEARTBEAT

Week 8 is often the week of confirmation. Typically, when you discover your partner is pregnant, the doctors won't always do the first ultrasound until the eighth week of pregnancy. The goal is to give the baby enough time to develop closer to a fetus than an embryo (roughly ten weeks).

Week 8 is likely the moment you've been waiting for. This will be the first time where you and your partner are going to see—and more importantly *hear*—your baby. There's a lot to go over in that first meeting with the doctor, however, let's just focus on the most prominent thing—the ultrasound.

You sit down beside your partner, look at a blank black screen, and suddenly, you see that small movement of grey right where it should be.

"And that's *your* baby. You are, indeed, pregnant."

It's a crazy moment to experience, and a beautiful one too. To finally receive confirmation that something is actually in there, that it's growing. It's hard to put to words. However, what's even better is the next moment where they direct you to the first sound your baby makes for you—their heartbeat.

That extra-fast *thump-thump-thump-thump*. Often nearly 160 beats per minute.

Whew, it really is something special.

REFLECTIONS FROM OUR DADS

"For a few weeks after you first see the pregnancy test, you're like, okay, she's pregnant, awesome. But you almost aren't convinced. Then, once you hear that heartbeat, and see them on the screen it's like—wow, this is real."
— Cole F. North Carolina, US.

"I constantly thought about and wondered how he's going to turn out and how personality is going to be shaped."
- Matteo V. Surrey, UK

"When I first saw the baby in the scan. I remember that feeling so clearly. Your heart skips a beat. I knew it was coming but I didn't expect to see it so fast! It was amazing to see how formed it already was."
- Fred S. London, UK.

"My partner being pregnant was the catalyst for me to get therapy – to sort out some issues. There was a lot of clutter in my mind that I wanted to sort. A lot of it was driven by my own experiences with my father, that needed some help to get clarity on as I was about to be a dad myself."
- Robin L. London, UK.

☑ WEEKLY CHECKLIST

☐ Your first prenatal ultrasound! (Likely eight or nine weeks).

☐ This will often cover your partner's weight, blood pressure, and urine in addition to seeing the baby and hearing that lovely heartbeat.

☐ Ask your doctor about when the next appointment should be.

☐ They might recommend genetic testing as an option during the next appointment (we'll go over that in more detail in Week 11).

CHAPTER THREE

MONTH THREE

The last month of the first trimester is the one that really shows pregnancy isn't a sprint, it's a marathon. This is also the month where it dawns on most dads that even if the nine months feels quick when you look back on it, the days can sometimes feel far longer when you're in the thick of it. *One step at a time*, that's how you should take it.

Your partner might be having some extreme morning sickness along with any other symptoms from the past month—and a couple of new ones, including some pretty intense headaches. However, it's also common for many women not to feel these early pregnancy symptoms, and that's entirely fine too.

Fortunately, as far as morning sickness is concerned, many women feel the severity of it lessen in the second trimester. But just so you're aware, it's not entirely uncommon for morning sickness to last throughout pregnancy, and sometimes it can seem like hiccups—once it's gone, your partner is left wondering if it will start up again. Whatever the symptoms, try to stay supportive and involved. Positive thinking is *always* a benefit in the present.

A lot is happening with your baby this month, and month three is where they really start to take on their "baby" shape. By the end, they'll have developed intestines and a functioning musculature system. Their bones will harden, even if their spine is still pretty soft by comparison. On the outside, the baby will start to show little fingers and toes wiggling on the ultrasound—and on those fingers and toes, little nails just starting to grow. Finally, in month three external genitalia are starting to grow, allowing predictions of gender early in the second trimester.

You might be surprised how quickly this stage has reached you but just remember and repeat it like a mantra: *one step at a time.* You're doing great so far!

99

WEEK 9

HEAD, SHOULDERS, KNEES & TOES

TERMS TO KNOW

Reproductive System – The male (testes) or female (ovaries) and all the connected pieces involved in creating babies.

Testes – Male reproductive organs, the prizes to our cash, the berries to our twig—these two organs are where sperm is produced in men (and they really hurt to get kicked).

Ovaries – Female reproductive organs where eggs are produced.

MOTHER AND BABY

Your lovely little olive is welcoming you to your third month (.09 inches & .07 ounces)! That's right, nearly an inch long, your baby is now the perfect accent to a James Bond martini (even if he liked a lemon peel for the Vesper.) Either way, your baby is looking more like a baby every day, and the placenta is now producing all the progesterone needed for pregnancy. Before, your partner's ovaries were still the main producers of this powerful hormone, but now that the placenta has taken its full shape, it's sending all the vital nutrients to your baby, the embryo.

Your baby is also making another huge leap: they are now big enough that the umbilical cord no longer houses intestines, and they're funnelling their way into the abdomen. To add to that, their face is really defining its shape, and your baby now has taste buds! That's right, and they're going to begin to react to what your partner is feeding them. Spicy, sugary, or plant-based goodness, baby's palette will start to form based on your partner's eating habits.

The last big thing to mention with Week 9 is the sex of the baby. Either the testes or ovaries are settling into place and beginning to form (something doctors will be able to check very soon.) Here's a crazy fact: if it happens to be ovaries, they're already filled to the brim with all the eggs your daughter will have for the rest of her life.

A quick side note, by the time females start their period, they'll have about 350,000 to 450,000 eggs—and will lose about 1,000 a month as they age. Just like brain cells, eggs don't come back—so what the baby has now is the bank account fully loaded.

Understandably, this sounds like a lot happening in just one week. And it is. As far as your partner goes, she'll be feeling it. Even if she can't yet feel the baby moving around, morning sickness usually peaks in week nine or in the following week. Don't worry, this is good news! After the peak, hopefully things level out for your partner, and those bouts of sickness can feel on a steady decline rather than more prevalent.

If you're unsure how to help support your partner through this time, she'll always appreciate a fresh glass of water (or some other favorite non-alcoholic drink!) And while you're at it, another added symptom of Week 9 is increased mucus production, so maybe have a tissue handy too!

WHAT'S HAPPENING WITH YOU - COVID STRESS

We know it can seem like there's a lot to worry about during pregnancy. Stress can creep its way into our lives in any number of ways, and sometimes it feels like it can find *even more* ways once there's a baby on the way.

As of this writing, a big stressor for first-time dads is the effects of COVID-19. There's still a lot of questions as to the long-term effects of the pandemic on pregnant women—right now, studies have linked it to some cases of pre-term birth and other complications. However, the important thing to remember about COVID is the same for almost *everything* pregnancy-related.

Have you ever seen that little warning label on nearly every medicine that says: "Do not take if you are pregnant or . . ." You've seen those messages everywhere for your entire life, but they finally connect with *you*.

The reason there are a lot of pregnancy warnings on different items is because a lot of things can impact the development of the baby: alcohol, smoking, deli meats leading to *Listeria* (bacteria from contaminated food), or raw eggs leading to *Salmonella* (bacteria that can cause food poisoning). All of these things are *always* a danger to anyone's health, but a baby lacks immunity and resistance to these things—they're more susceptible, so it can increase the chances of miscarriage or developmental issues.

In that way, COVID-19 is another thing we're adapting to with pregnancy. It's not something to keep you up at night wrought with worry, but it's another on the long list of things to be conscious of. Just as with all those other things, do your best to limit the possibility of infection, which you were likely *already* doing.

But more than just ourselves, COVID is something we're evolving and adapting to as a society. As we mentioned before, many dads were locked out of the delivery room because of COVID restrictions, and many mothers weren't allowed to have skin-to-skin contact with their newborns for fear of infection. These regulations have changed or been reduced in the past months, but the effects of COVID have fundamentally altered how we, as a society, see things and react.

In the coming months and years, we might experience a new variant that brings about a new vaccine, and there may be times with high infection rates where restrictions are put in place once more. Whatever the case, know that there are options, and as individuals and a society we'll navigate those options. When it comes to your baby, we understand the stress COVID can add, but the good news is we now have a plethora of cases and experience to look back on so that we have better answers and better solutions.

REFLECTIONS FROM OUR DADS

"A lot of times, the pregnancy feels like a series of checks and balances. We check in on each other pretty constantly—I'm constantly asking, 'how are you feeling?' And if we're on the same page, the scales feel balanced. Even if the other scale keeps steadily creeping up for both of us."
— James G. California, US.

"I didn't think morning sickness would be so intense so quickly! Everyday for a period of weeks, she could only eat toast and marmite because it was the only thing she seemed to keep down!"
- Louis M. Surrey,UK.

"There was this dawning sense of having this new responsibility and no escape. There's no walking away. This is it, forever."
- Adam I. London, UK.

"COVID has really had an impact on work and travel during the pregnancy. I've been away on deployment and because of surges we just haven't felt safe having her travel, even with the vaccine. It's tough, but we take it day by day and video calls have been an amazing help."
- Dean F. Kansas, US.

☑ WEEKLY CHECKLIST

☐ Talk to your partner about the many types of
birth available (i.e., natural, vaginal, induction,
water, c-section) to see which one works best
for you both or which you'd like to learn more
about—there are a lot of options out there!

☐ Eat with her—if she's eating more, maybe join in and unwind a
bit.

☐ Do some research on local hospitals or midwives:
   ☐ Start reaching out and making calls.
   ☐ Remember, you don't have to settle for the first place you
   had an appointment—find what works for both of you!

WEEK 10

FROM EMBRYO TO FETUS

MOTHER AND BABY

Boom! The baby levelled up from embryo to *fetus*. Next step . . . well . . . *baby!* Technically infant, but from now on we're going to be tracking fetal development rather than embryonic development and that's exciting! The big defining factor of a fetus is that all those vital internal organs are now *inside* the baby because there's plenty of space for them to start growing. And now the most important organ, the heart, is a four-chambered, blood-pumping machine that is way more complex than the simple tube it started as only a few weeks ago. That's some serious progress!

This is all made crazier because the baby is literally as long as *your thumb* and about as wide as a strawberry (1.2 inches and .14 ounces). They are covered in translucent skin, and growing tiny hairs called *lanugo*, which will help regulate their temperature (more on that later). Because the skin is translucent, you could also feasibly see the baby's bones starting to grow and connect (although it is much more cartilage than bone at this point).  But how's this for mind-boggling: your baby now has more bones than you do! That right, your baby has around 270 bones in their little body, whereas an average adult has 206. As your baby continues to develop, those bones will start to fuse together until they have 206 too.

To change gears back to your partner, all this growing could be starting to really impact her sleep cycle. During Week 10, many mothers-to-be experience some nighttime restlessness and feel extremely exhausted during the day. This has a lot to do with blood flow as their bodies are producing more blood to send to the fetus. To add to that, their blood vessels are getting wider to facilitate this, which can lower their own blood pressure making them feel tired, or even sometimes feel faint.

The other effect on sleeping is that all this increased progesterone and other hormones, along with the roller-coaster of pregnancy in general, can make your partner experience some wild, off-the-rails, and vivid (sometimes sexy, eyyy-oh!) dreams. Dreams happen to us during REM (rapid eye movement) sleep and often by the time we wake up, we often forget them. But because your partner is waking up so often to pee or from discomfort throughout the night, those dreams are more easily remembered.

So yeah, there might be a lot of nightmare-running from crab people with roller-skates on their feet . . . or worse, work dreams. The horror!!

WHAT'S HAPPENING WITH YOU - SEX & PREGNANCY

Since we've already brought up the possibility of some sexy dreams, it's a good time to address a big concern for first-time dads: *sex during pregnancy*. Don't worry, we will have another section covering sex after the baby is born, but let's focus on the pregnancy for now.

As we've mentioned before, hormones during pregnancy impact women in many different ways. It's possible your partner (assuming you had a romantic relationship together) had a very high libido (sex drive) before the pregnancy but hasn't been in the mood ever since its begun. On the other hand, some women experience the opposite and have a greatly increased sex drive during pregnancy.

There's no way to predict how hormones will affect your partner, but we can tell you that it tends to fluctuate throughout the pregnancy. Sometimes, women who experience severe morning sickness in the first trimester can also have severe cramping that accompany orgasms. Sometimes the super sense of smell and other more visceral connections of pregnant women to their bodies makes sex more enjoyable. Sometimes they simply have no drive for sex early on, but fortunately, most have their libido return in the second trimester.

The bottom line is that sexual relationships can be directly impacted by pregnancy. However, it's not only how it affects your partner, but you as well. Some men feel scared to have sex while their partner is pregnant because they are nervous about impacting the baby. Try not to worry about that. You won't "poke the baby," and the cervical mucus protects it from any ejaculate before it even gets to the amniotic sac. To squash another myth, you very, very, very likely won't re-impregnate your partner when she is already pregnant. *Superfetation* is what it's called, and it's extremely rare; only a handful of cases exist in *all* of our documented medical literature. However, a much more pressing anxiety can be that some men feel too much stress during pregnancy to find themselves in the mood. As it goes, there's no quick resolution for all the stressors you may be experiencing, but you can at least put the anxieties about the dangers of sex during pregnancy to rest. Barring any concerns from your doctors, **sex is safe while pregnant**—just be mindful of positions.

If either you or your partner aren't feeling up to it, the best thing you can do is be patient with each other. There's a lot going on, so be kind and empathetic with yourself and your partner. You might just need time to get used to the new changes unfolding in your lives. And odds are, if your partner has been throwing up all day, or simply feels exhausted, there is not much you can do to get them in the mood. But don't give up! These moments can still be an opportunity for different types of romantic connection and intimacy—cuddling, bonding, or just sharing time together in this exciting journey.

More than anything else, talk to your partner if you feel like your sexual relationship is becoming a concern for you, or for her.

REFLECTIONS FROM OUR DADS

"Our sex life didn't change too drastically during pregnancy, but we started finding new ways to enjoy each other's company when we were just too tired, or she felt too sick. Sometimes that just meant laying together and making plans for the future with our baby."
— Thomas M. Florida, US.

"There was huge excitement once we found out. It brought up a lot of thoughts about the future, and definitely gave me a clear sense of purpose. It's quite amazing how your mind shifts very quickly when you realize there's going to be a dependant relying on you in the future."
- Keneal P. London, UK.

"The morning sickness of the first trimester for my wife was pretty severe. We didn't really have sex very often, but the second trimester felt like a switch flipped. It was honestly a great time for both of us."
— Emmanuel V. Texas, US.

☑ WEEKLY CHECKLIST

☐ Confirm the Week 12 follow-up appointment with your doctor is in the calendar!

☐ Start thinking about some maternity clothes as potential gifts, or maybe plan a fun shopping trip (or make the budget for them).

☐ Follow up or reach out to your insurance provider to see what is covered, the possible deductible, and what isn't covered with regards to prenatal support, labor and delivery, and postpartum care.

WEEK 11

TEETH & MAYBE BABY BUMPS

TERMS TO KNOW

Genetic Blood Testing – Optional test of mother's blood to screen for abnormalities with the baby's DNA.

Palpation – Pressing on the abdomen to examine fetus through touch and feel.

NT Scan – A nuchal translucency scan screens for the possibility of Down Syndrome.

Down Syndrome – A genetic chromosomal disorder that occurs from an error in division resulting in extra chromosome 21. It often causes developmental and intellectual delays.

Sickle Cell Anemia – An inherited disease that changes the shape of red blood cells to a "sickle shape," making them easier to break down.

Cystic Fibrosis - A hereditary disorder that affects exocrine glands, causing an excess build-up of thick mucus that can affect the respiratory system.

MOTHER AND BABY

Your baby is already the size of a lime (1.6 inches and .25 ounces), but there's still no way to predict when your partner will start to "show." Some women start to show as early as ten weeks, and second-time mothers might show even sooner. No matter

when it arrives, that little baby bump can start to affect your partner psychologically, either positively or negatively (or both). They might be over the moon to have a daily reminder, or it might make them more nervous, having something that sometimes feels "foreign" growing inside of them. After all, *seeing is believing*, and the time between ultrasounds or heartbeat readings can sometimes feel like an eternity.

Your baby is all about the teeth this week, as they are not only developing the buds for their baby teeth but also their adult teeth. That's right, their mouth comes prepared for those pearly whites and the first batch of ten baby teeth on top and ten on the bottom. Just enough to chow down on a nice home-cooked meal (much later of course)!

Besides the teeth and the fully formed face, your baby's blood vessels are working like the *Little Engine That Could* to pump blood beneath their translucent skin. And as far as the feet and hands go, they're dividing more and more which means wiggling, making fists, and stretching out those toes.

Besides the psychological impact of the bump, your partner might be experiencing some leg cramps added to the mix of symptoms.

YOU'RE GOING TO BE A DAD!

Hopefully, the morning sickness is easing off, but leg cramps are often a result of the baby using up a lot of your partner's potassium and magnesium stores. There are supplements for both, and the prenatal supplement will likely have them—but a banana or banana smoothie can really help with potassium. And happy days, dark chocolate also has quite a bit of magnesium!

You're welcome.

WHAT'S HAPPENING WITH YOU - GENETIC TESTING

Over the course of the pregnancy, it can feel like there's a barrage of appointments and rapid decisions to make. In the first trimester, one of the earliest decisions is optional genetic testing or genetic screening.

The reason for genetic testing is to help the doctors look for any missing, defective, or additional genes within the baby. This information is used to determine if the baby has certain medical conditions that might need to be addressed or if they potentially have a known genetic disorder, such as Down Syndrome, which is the primary condition they test for in the first trimester. However, in most cases, a baby would only receive an inherited disorder (like sickle cell anemia or cystic fibrosis) if both parents carried the same mutated gene.

In the first trimester, there's an option for genetic testing between Weeks 10 and 14. In the second trimester, there are further options for testing between Weeks 15 and 22. The important thing to remember about these optional screenings is that they both come with a time limit—if your partner crosses these thresholds during her pregnancy, it's likely your doctors won't perform them. However, it should also be noted that as advancements continue all the time in the medical world, the methods of testing are becoming more refined and efficient.

Genetic testing is an important conversation to have with your partner early in the pregnancy. There are no right or wrong answers, but it's still one of the earliest choices you'll have to make!

REFLECTIONS FROM OUR DADS

"I think that's always one of the biggest fears early on in pregnancy, having a kid with special needs. It sucks to be worried about challenges they might face, but it doesn't make you love them any less. The longer the pregnancy goes on, the closer you become to your baby, and the less any of that matters."
— Kevin H. Utah, US.

"We did do the genetic testing, and it was sort of a mixed bag. It caused some relief and some worry. In hindsight, the worry was worth the time."
— James G. California, US

"We actually skipped the screening. We figured whatever it told us wasn't worth knowing for us. Some people want to, and I totally understand. We just knew it wouldn't change anything knowing the results."
— Taylor W. Washington, US

"Because of COVID, I didn't get to go to any of the scans. My partner had to go on her own for the Down Syndrome tests. I remember looking at the phone and thinking — "I just need that to ring and tell me everything was fine." It was horrible not being able to go in. I just sat in a café — in that initial part, while she was being assessed."
- Rob S, York, UK.

☑ WEEKLY CHECKLIST

☐ Talk with your partner about optional genetic testing (you'll likely hear more about it at the Week 12 doctor's visit).

   ☐ The Chorionic *Villus Sampling* or CVS looks for chromosomal problems and other genetic abnormalities (given between weeks 10 and 13).

   ☐ The *Nuchal Translucency Scan* looks for abnormalities related to Down Syndrome (given between weeks 11 and 14).

☐ Think about letting your work or anyone applicable know about your baby!

ANYTHING TO EAT AROUND HERE?

TERMS TO KNOW

Metabolism – The body's process of turning food into energy (metabolic rate is how well it does that).

Thyroid – Gland that releases hormones that play a huge role in metabolism.

Electrolytes – Minerals like sodium, potassium, and magnesium, all of which are super important for muscle function and hydration.

MOTHER AND BABY

It's Week 12, and the baby has already doubled in size from the previous week! From crown to rump, they are now the size of a billiard ball (2.1 inches and .49 ounces)!

By Week 12, we're *technically* at the end of the third month! But not according to the baby—we still have one more week to finish out the first trimester. This is also probably a good time to mention that there is some debate in the medical world as to when the trimesters begin and end. There's usually about a week's difference between various opinions, but for some reason, the only thing most doctors agree on is that the third trimester begins at 28 weeks. The big reason for the debate is something we can't help but repeat: **babies call the shots, and time is relative to them!**

That said, the biggest milestone of Week 12 are reflexes. Your baby is now starting to experiment with what their brain stem is offering them. They're moving their mouth and rounding it to prepare for breastfeeding. They're also yawning, swallowing some amniotic fluid, and starting to use the uterus as their own personal gym! *Okay,* that isn't always the case, but babies can often be very active at 12 weeks. They just got their fingers and toes; now they have to see what those babies (no pun intended) can do!

On the plus side, Week 12 also typically marks your first follow-up meeting with the doctor, which often gives you another chance to see your baby on the ultrasound and hear that beautiful heartbeat.

Hearing this incredible sound can offer a little peace of mind to you and your partner, and it's also (hopefully) compounded with some lessening symptoms of morning sickness. However, your partner might also experience some dizziness this week. Hormone shifts and changes to blood pressure (as the baby is demanding more blood flow) might cause some lightheadedness. The best fix for this is typically lying down, but snacking often (especially on something a little saltier or full of electrolytes) can sometimes help too.

One other thing to remind you of is that your partner might experience some leukorrhea discharge. As long as it's white, clearish, and relatively odorless, there's no reason to panic. Discharge can be common throughout pregnancy at differing times—the times to ask questions to your doctors are when spotting turns into a heavier flow, or if the discharge looks abnormal (yellow, brownish, or has a strong odor).

WHAT'S HAPPENING WITH YOU - THE EXERCISE GRIND

Around this time in pregnancy, many women are starting to feel some energy return to them. It's not always the case, however, as fatigue can be pervasive throughout pregnancy for some women and for others not really be much of a symptom at all.

Regardless of whether you and your partner have been in a regimen of physical activity from the beginning, this might be a good week to check out what activities sound approachable for you. Going to hit the gym at four in the morning, pumping some iron for three hours, and then topping it off with a crazy cardio circuit might be pushing it, but exploring a few options for gentle physical activity can be great for you and your partner. Just like nutrition, exercise can benefit the baby's development and is an added stress reliever. Of course, you never want to *overdo* it—but some daily activity (and some sunshine if it's available) can be a great way to unwind and break a sweat.

There are a number of great pregnancy workouts out there, and most focus on bodyweight exercises or light resistance. However, what's possible (or even enjoyable) will entirely depend on your partner. If that isn't something you're looking for, yoga is a great option to take together, along with a good old-fashioned stroll around the neighborhood or local park. As an added bonus, walking is a good opportunity to bond over the baby and build some healthy habits. Who knows, charting a nice walking path might even be a fun plan for a future with strollers!

REFLECTIONS FROM OUR DADS

"It's kind of funny, I used to mountain bike almost every day and it was when we were trying to conceive. After we actually found out we were pregnant, suddenly I come across an article on 5 Worst Things to Do When Trying, and there it is, mountain biking. Whoops. Ah well, it worked out."
— Cole F. North Carolina, US.

"I found myself being very regimental – like I'm training an athlete – with the right vitamins and that sort of thing."
- Ameet H. London, UK

"My main worry after previous miscarriage was that there would be issues, so that first 12 week scan coming back good was a real high, and a relief too!"
- Adam I. London, UK

☑ WEEKLY CHECKLIST

☐ Your second prenatal appointment!

  ☐ Often will review the results of the previous appointment to let you know anything to be conscious of like the possibility of being a high-risk pregnancy and genetic testing.

  ☐ Ask your doctor about any vaccine recommendations or information—especially the COVID-19 vaccination and flu shot.

☐ Schedule your next prenatal appointment, possibly the *20-week Anatomy Scan.*

☐ If your partner is still exercising, make sure they've got fully supportive footwear and clothing.

  ☐ There are some great pregnancy-safe athletic shoes made to slide on without having to bend down (immensely helpful in later trimesters).

  ☐ They may also be using this stage to enroll in pregnancy yoga, Pilates, or another group or at-home program— some classes you could potentially take together!

FIRST TRIMESTER DONE!

TERMS TO KNOW

Migraines – A recurring, throbbing, and truly horrible headache.

Urinary System – Parts of the body designed to get rid of waste, such as the kidneys, bladder, ureters, and urethra.

Ureters – Little duct that connects the kidney to the bladder so urine can move through.

MOTHER AND BABY

A whole inch of growth in just one week brings your baby to almost three inches—right about the size of a pea pod! (2.9 inches and .81 ounces) And speaking of a "pee" pod, the baby is likely starting to make a little bit of urine in the womb too as they test out their urinary system. In that way, the baby is a bit like a goldfish, relieving itself in the amniotic fluid and then "breathing" in and recycling that fluid in all its glory. Go green! As a quick side note, "breathing" in that fluid actually helps to develop the baby's lungs later on.

Okay, so it's not *entirely* like a goldfish. We have to clean a fishbowl while the baby frolics freely and happily within their own nutritious urine without a care in the world.

Bear Grylls, eat your heart out.

Wait, don't actually. That wasn't a dare, Bear. Stop!

Anyway, Week 13 marks a significant milestone as it's the end of the first trimester! However, it may not feel all that amazing to your partner, as she might now be experiencing a fairly common symptom of the end of the trimester: *migraines*.

Pregnancy migraines, like any migraine, are no joke—a headache so severe that it can stop your partner in her tracks. We hope they're not a symptom of your partner's pregnancy. However, if they are, try to analyze what foods might be triggering it, focus on getting sleep, and if medication is needed, be sure to ask your doctor which ones work best!

WHAT'S HAPPENING WITH YOU - MILESTONES & ANNOUNCEMENTS

Week 13 is the end of the first trimester, and it's pretty insane that it's already here. It's a milestone worth celebrating, one of many you'll encounter during the pregnancy. And speaking of celebrating, the end of the first trimester is also a common time when couples think about *announcing the pregnancy*. It is by no means mandatory, of course, and many people have reservations about announcing early—or announcing at all.

Much like sharing the news with family and close friends, announcing a pregnancy should only happen on your timeline. Some people like to take pictures with the ultrasound to announce their baby, while some like to keep the whole thing private. Some choose to announce at thirteen weeks or earlier, and some wait until well into the second or third trimester. There's no official timeline—it's really just what you're comfortable with and what plans you might have personally for the pregnancy. This is wonderful news though, and it feels amazing to share it with whoever you'd like to!

REFLECTIONS FROM OUR DADS

"My wife was so excited to announce. I think it was around fifteen weeks, but she's a flight attendant, and she tracked the flight routes for planes landing and her best friend took the picture with it right over our heads. Not going to lie, it felt pretty epic. More than that, it just felt amazing to finally share the news!"
— David R. North Carolina, US.

"I definitely felt like I'd matured over the first few weeks. I feel a bit more matured into having those responsibilities."
- Louis M. Surrey, UK.

"Those three months can feel like they go by so fast. You're running around, working and planning, and all the while your baby is just in there, growing and experiencing new things every day. It's crazy to think about."
— James P. Ohio, US.

"My wife had a short cervix (the average is 25mm, and my wife's is 15 mm). So she had to have a surgery to help keep the baby up there. We were warned that if we didn't have it we'd miscarry by 24 weeks. The recovery has come along fine, but it's certainly been another thing to worry about!"
- Fred S. London, UK.

☑ WEEKLY CHECKLIST

☐ Celebrate one trimester in the books!

☐ Start researching some big baby purchases like strollers, cribs, and car seats to start budgeting—or create a registry to get help from family and friends.

☐ Talk to your partner about the possibility of a pregnancy announcement!

☐ If you've got the time and a budget for it, start thinking about planning a fun trip—sometimes called a *Babymoon* where you and your partner can get away for a bit before the baby arrives and definitely before it becomes too difficult to travel.

PART TWO

THE SECOND TRIMESTER

The second trimester covers Week 14 to the end of Week 27, and for most women, this is the most enjoyable (tolerable) part of pregnancy. In a lot of cases, gone are the days of overwhelming morning sickness and discomfort of the first trimester, and the days of added weight in the third trimester are still months away. This in no way means that the second trimester is a breeze (or any part of pregnancy, for that matter), but on the whole, it's when you both can really find your bearings again.

While the second trimester still has its hurdles, the foundation for both baby and your pregnant partner have been laid, and you yourself might be feeling a little more comfortable with everything that's going on. The second trimester will also mark the halfway point of the pregnancy at twenty weeks, and it will be the first time your partner might feel some of those famous baby kicks, which at this point might feel more like butterflies in her stomach.

Beyond that, the second trimester will also offer you some key insights into how your baby is developing. There may be tests performed to determine gender, another optional genetic screening, and the twenty-week anatomy scan. We'll get into what all this information means in the coming chapters, and what decisions can be made to help you better prepare.

CHAPTER FOUR

MONTH FOUR

With one-third of the pregnancy in the rearview, the fourth month can often feel like a welcome change of pace from the sickness and constant bodily changes of the previous three. Also, as a fun little side note, sometimes women experience thicker and shinier hair as a result of pregnancy this month.

Thank goodness, not all negative symptoms!

While your partner's body is still changing every day—growing, expanding, and providing nutrition—the groundwork is set, and the upkeep will hopefully feel a little less strenuous. Her hormones might still be a little out of sync, but she is likely getting a reprieve from nausea and the intense smells. And because of all these changes, many women will also feel a return of their usual energy—perhaps even a return of their sex drive that may have dissipated in the first trimester.

Just as before, your baby is growing like crazy over these next weeks, developing new organs and refining ones that have been around for a while now. By the end of this month, the baby will more than double in size—and that means your partner might see the first semblance of their lovely "baby bump!"

WEEK 14

PEACH-FUZZ & FACIAL EXPRESSIONS

TERMS TO KNOW

Fundal Height – Method for doctors to measure baby's growth from the outside by charting the distance from pelvis to the top of your partner's belly button.

Gestational Age – How far along your partner and baby are in pregnancy (could be different than expected).

Wharton's Jelly – Jelly-like substance that provides insulation and protection for the umbilical cord.

Inferior Vena Cava – Large vein carrying blood to the heart. Pregnancy can increase pressure on the vein thanks to the growing baby and lying down.

MOTHER AND BABY

It's Week 14, and your baby is the size of a peach! (3.4 inches and 1.5 ounces) Like a peach, your baby's peach-fuzz (lanugo) is growing EVERYWHERE. That light, fluffy hair is sprouting up all over and will disappear shortly before birth. However, what's really big for the baby this week is practicing more reflexes and facial expressions.

These aren't necessarily responses to *anything* just yet, but they are now learning how to frown, smile, or grimace in angst-like anger at your taste in music. A great precursor to the teen years. Your baby is also moving their hands and feet, using their fingers to grasp whatever they can—most often the umbilical cord. Don't worry, though. Even though the cord is the baby's lifeline, the thick protective *Wharton's Jelly* that covers it means they're nowhere near strong enough to do any damage to it with their light squeezes, and finger stretches.

As we mentioned earlier, your partner's symptoms will hopefully be lessening in intensity this week. Of course, not all women will see early pregnancy symptoms drop away at the onset of the second trimester, but this week usually marks the start of feeling a little better—or, at least, a little more comfortable. But while some symptoms like nausea are placed on the back burner, other symptoms like acid reflux may be on the rise and further impacted by diet decisions. Surprisingly, this doesn't always mean that a woman's body will naturally crave a healthy salad or rich fruit smoothie— sometimes the things they can stomach happen to be exclusively *Taco Bell*.

The tough part in that situation is *how do we support our partner* when they're craving food that might give them negative symptoms like heartburn or acid reflux? Unfortunately, the real crux of it is that stress and not eating can have a more negative effect on a pregnant woman than most anything else. In that way, your partner might be craving food that isn't great for the baby or for her, but eating something is often better than not eating at all. It's a difficult fence to balance on, and you won't always fall on the healthy side. However, reducing stress is paramount. If this time your partner gets *Taco Bell* as a last-minute option, maybe try to be proactive and offer alternatives next time.

To add to that, you might also notice big swings in your partner's appetite. They might have insatiable new cravings, or they might have less of an appetite than they did in the previous trimester. As a basic rule, your baby is consuming a lot more of your partner's calories than previously. That being said, "eating for two" doesn't mean eating double the food, but rather double the **quality** of food than previously. On average, a woman needs about 2,000 calories per day, but a baby will only consume roughly 300 calories per day. Because of that, a pregnant woman is encouraged to increase her caloric intake, but not to 4,000 calories a day—likely only about 300-600 calories more.

You can't always encourage your partner to eat more or less, but it's a good idea to have snacks they enjoy around—and some for you too!

WHAT'S HAPPENING WITH YOU - SLEEP CYCLES THROUGH THE TRIMESTERS

It's best that we talk about it as early as possible, but your partner's sleep patterns (and, indeed, yours) are likely to change throughout the pregnancy. They are *definitely* going to change once your baby joins the world, but that's still quite a way off—and we'll talk more about that later on.

But for now, a lot of pregnant women find sleep to be a little evasive. Almost 50% of all pregnant women have claimed to experience insomnia. Some pregnant women experience restless leg syndrome (RLS, uncontrollable leg movement), others obstructive sleep apnea (OSA, basically a lot of snoring), and others acid reflux and heartburn, which makes getting comfortable at night pretty tough.

Right now, just shy of fifteen weeks into the pregnancy, it's possible that your partner is encountering yet another hurdle that gets in the way of a good night's sleep as the baby is now big enough to put pressure on your partner's *inferior vena cava blood vessel.* This means that your partner's blood flow can be impacted on its return to the heart when lying on their back for too long (whether resting, exercising, or otherwise). Because of that, pregnant women are encouraged to start sleeping on their side—specifically their left side, which helps reduce pressure on the vena cava and increases circulation.

If your partner is used to sleeping on her back, or even her stomach, this might be when the doctors encourage them to make the switch. But if you spend your whole life sleeping one way, it doesn't necessarily feel great to change up the program. To help out with that, you can buy your partner a large pregnancy body pillow, which looks like a giant unrolled pretzel. They are extremely comfortable and become even more comfortable as your partner's baby bump continues to round out. If it's in the budget, it might make a great gift for you too!

Beyond pregnancy symptoms, it's also likely that the baby will start messing with your partner's sleep schedule. As the baby (and, in turn, the uterus that surrounds the baby) continues to expand, they can both put a lot of pressure on your partner's bladder. That not only means frequent bathroom breaks during the day, but also waking up at night to pee. If you're a light sleeper, that might affect you too.

There are some helpful preventative measures, thankfully, and they're worth trying out. Your partner can drink lots of water during the day but then stop a few hours before bed, or she can avoid heavy meals at night to help prevent acid reflux or heartburn. But the best advice is simply getting into a solid routine that makes sleep a priority rather than an afterthought. Sleep, across all trimesters of pregnancy, is vital for your baby's development and both you and your partner's physical health and mental health. Simply do your best to make sleep a priority, but above all, be gentle and compassionate with yourself and your partner. Remember, you're a team!

REFLECTIONS FROM OUR DADS

"My wife used to say that whenever she was sleeping is where the baby felt most active—her exact words were, 'She just did another pile-driver on my bladder.' Sometimes she'd go to the bathroom five times a night."
— Carson D. Melbourne, AUS.

"Not going to lie, those pregnancy pillows are *really* comfortable. My girlfriend uses it at night, but it's perfect for chilling on the couch."
— Emmanuel V. Texas, US.

"There were a few of emotional outbursts. And I get it - a pregnancy is emotionally charged, but it can sometimes catch you off guard."
- Keneal P. London, UK.

☑ WEEKLY CHECKLIST

☐ Find a pregnancy pillow for your partner (and maybe you too!).

☐ Try to create an open dialogue with your partner about the changes the pregnancy may already be bringing:

    ☐ *Sex* - how the drives may fluctuate for both of you during pregnancy. Many women feel a return in libido in the second trimester, but that isn't always the case. Embrace where you are and find ways to be intimate.

    ☐ *Food* – cravings may shift, some smells may still repulse or maybe jumping on a good wellness and health plan hasn't been easy.

☐ Focus on the two of you as a team!

BUTTERFLIES IN DISGUISE

TERMS TO KNOW

Bone Ossification – Baby's bones start to harden by adding calcium to cartilage.

"Pregnancy Brain" – Typically refers to lapses in attention and memory—poorly represented but part of the brain's process of readying itself for a baby.

Gray Matter – The darker tissue of the brain and spinal cord, home of a lot of neural activity.

MOTHER AND BABY

Not so long ago your baby was the size of a seed, but now here they are at Week 15 nearly the size of an apple at 4 inches and 2.5 ounces! With such a big change in size, this week marks a milestone in pregnancy for two reasons.

The first is *bone ossification*—it's a big phrase, but all it means is that baby is finally able to convert all of its cartilage into bone by adding calcium into the mix. This can also impact your partner's calcium reserves, as the baby needs to get it from somewhere. We'll go more into that later, as the baby isn't taking an extreme amount of calcium just yet. However, with that hardening of bones beneath the growing muscles, every movement of the baby is now far more refined and sometimes able to be felt.

With that, this week might also mark the first time your partner can feel the baby moving. It might not be a kick quite yet, but these little movements, bounces, and stretches of the baby's growing limbs can feel a lot like butterflies in your partner's stomach. Actually, this early on, some women report that the baby flutters feel like gas bubbles (kind of like a fart you just can't quite let out), and it's pretty easy to confuse the two. But either way, these little butterfly flutters or gas bubbles will grow into a "flopping fish" of movement soon enough. If your partner isn't feeling those movements just yet, not to worry. It can start up anytime over the course of the second trimester.

More than strong bones or butterflies, the baby is also swallowing more of that amniotic fluid into their upper respiratory tract—a process that helps build their lungs. This fantastic feat further emphasizes just how important every process is in developing a baby and how absolutely *nothing* is wasted—not even waste! Every thirty minutes or so the baby's bladder contracts to expel urine into the amniotic fluid, which will then be recycled as we talked about in week 13.

Returning to your partner, they might also be feeling some of the new second-trimester pregnancy symptoms. These can vary, and they still might come in combination with lingering symptoms from the first trimester. However, a few new ones in the mix are swollen gums, heartburn, and shortness of breath—but also a potentially increased sex drive, *so how do you like them apples?!*

For the swollen gums, it might be a good time for your partner to think about how recent her last dentist visit was. Checking in at the dentist can be very important during pregnancy as dental problems left unchecked, like gum disease, can be detrimental for the baby.

As for heartburn (and likely indigestion), it's a trial-and-error process to find out which foods are causing it. Have some antacids handy (a slight bonus is that they're also chock-full of calcium for bone ossification!)

Lastly, shortness of breath is typically a result of the baby putting pressure on the diaphragm and possibly the lungs, making deep breaths harder to come by. Unfortunately, this symptom will likely become more common as the pregnancy goes on. Encourage your partner to take it easy and definitely step in to do any heavy lifting!

WHAT'S HAPPENING WITH YOU - PREGNANCY BRAIN & YOU

"Pregnancy brain" typically encompasses bouts of forgetfulness, strange memory lapses, or just overall brain fog. However, conventional wisdom exaggerates how often, or to what degree, it actually happens.

First off, not all women experience "pregnancy brain," and pregnancy definitely doesn't make women "lose their brain." With that out of the way, there is actually quite a bit of scientific research on the topic.

When women become pregnant, as you've already experienced, their body goes through a number of hormonal and physical changes, and their brains are no exception (even down to the gray matter). No normal cognitive abilities are affected, nor will they be affected in the long term; instead, their brains actually tend to instinctively start to compartmentalize new information. What looks like bouts of forgetfulness is actually their brain's way of redirecting focus—preparing them to be more attuned to the needs of their baby. Their brain is prioritizing for them, placing the baby at the top of the list by literally blocking out stressors and ignoring information it doesn't think it needs (like where she left those car keys).

Although these are natural instincts for an expectant mother, it can also feel like an annoyance to your partner if they experience it. Sometimes it can also be hard for you, but awareness is the first step. You can prepare for a few lapses in memory and maybe some bouts of inattention by not taking any of it personally. It's just them working out some natural instincts that have evolved over thousands of years.

On the plus side, pregnancy brain may not only help your partner by making them more dialed into the demands of pregnancy, but it can also help *you* adapt (and build more patience) as you work together to figure things out.

REFLECTIONS FROM OUR DADS

"It was so crazy the first time my girlfriend said she really *felt* our baby in there. She almost immediately brought my hand to her belly, and we waited there probably a full minute before, sure enough, I felt this little movement—almost like a waterbed."
— John C. California, US.

"Sage advice, never eat the last Oreo with a pregnant woman around. She got so mad you'd think I burned the house down. But I just couldn't stop laughing...all the way to the grocery store, at midnight, to buy more. Worth it."
- Barrett E. Chicago, US

"My partner really complained about feeling 'foggy' a good bit in the second trimester. Surprisingly, going for walks as our sort of exercise of the day helped. Not sure if it was the sunlight or what, but it sort of became our daily routine."
— Carson W. Florida, US.

☑ WEEKLY CHECKLIST

☐ Make sure your next prenatal appointment is booked (likely the *20-week Anatomy Scan*) — remember check-ups are usually at least once a month throughout the second trimester.

☐ Learn and prepare to ask your doctor questions about *amniocentesis* – a procedure that extracts amniotic fluid to detect the possibility of Down Syndrome, sickle cell anemia, and more.

☐ Talk with your partner about the possibility of learning the sex of your baby, or if you even would like to know ahead of time.

16

FLUTTERS, SNACKS, & SLEEPING

TERMS TO KNOW

Gastroesophageal Reflux Disease (GERD) – This digestive issue can cause heartburn and acid reflux and is extremely common with pregnant women.

Pica – A phenomenon where a person craves food that isn't really food (or at least isn't nutritious). Sometimes can include cravings as odd as rocks, dirt, or paper.

MOTHER AND BABY

Week 16 continues on with some rapid baby development and also some rapid movement coming from your baby, who is now the size of an avocado (4.6 inches & 3.5 ounces)! At this stage, their heartbeat is somewhere between 150 and 180 bpm—basically a workout level. And as a workout, your little avocado is moving all around, bouncing, stretching, yawning, sucking their thumb, and turning your partner's uterus into their own personal gym.

The movements aren't too impactful yet, and even if the baby kicks, it probably won't be with enough force for your partner to feel it. However, by Week 16 you might notice how your partner's diet can elicit a response from the baby. That's right, your baby can start to *taste* the food mother is bringing down and even develop a palette from those tastes! That means  the 3 a.m. snacks too! Your partner might experience a little extra flutter from the baby for sweet-tooth cravings, or maybe even a few for green smoothies.

However, that isn't the only thing your partner might share with the baby this week. How your partner is feeling mentally can also impact how the baby is feeling. They may not be able to process those emotions yet, but physiological changes in the mother's psyche— from stress to happiness to anger—are starting to be felt by the baby as well. In that regard, doing anything you can to help lessen the stress and encourage a positive atmosphere isn't only helping the energy in the room, but also in the womb.

If your partner is experiencing a lot of heartburn or acid reflux this week, it might be a good time to ask your doctor about potential treatments for *gastroesophageal reflux disease* (GERD). It's often characterized as a more severe acid reflux, but the symptoms are similar. Some foods known to cause or make GERD more affecting are chocolate, mint, coffee, spicy foods, and foods with high acidity (like tomatoes and oranges).

Lastly, another common symptom that might start this week are nosebleeds. The increase of blood flow and blood volume in your partner might trigger them, but for the most part, there's no need to worry about it. It might, however, be a good idea to start strategically placing tissue boxes around the house.

WHAT'S HAPPENING WITH YOU - REGISTRIES, WORK, & BUDGETS

It's entirely possible that the pregnancy has already affected your work routine. Perhaps you've changed your schedule up a bit, or maybe focus is harder to come by as you deal with all the changes. Either way, it's best to let your employer (or anyone you feel necessary in your organization) know that you are expecting a baby. The sooner everyone is on the same page, the easier the planning will go.

We'll go into "taking leave from work" a little later on, but first, it's important to talk about the cost of pregnancy and how easily it can stack up if you're not careful. By now, even if you haven't decided on a doctor, midwife, or a birth facility, you've probably heard how much prenatal care, hospital stays, and things like a C-Section or anesthesia can cost (if you're going down the private insurance route).

If your insurance/healthcare is covering a majority of those expenses, it can be a real relief, but those aren't always the only costs, especially when accounting for deductibles.

We know, talking about hidden fees can bring on some anxiety, but money is often something looming on the minds of first-time dads:

"Do I make enough to support a baby financially?"

Without getting too far into the weeds, it's important to know that there are a lot of programs out there to help with pregnancy and delivery. It may take a fair bit of research about your unique situation, and some phone calls, but there are solutions to be found. That being said, budgeting usually works best when you know what to expect. Here are a few of the bigger practical purchases just for your baby that you should be keeping in mind too:

- Infant or adaptable stroller

- Infant car-seat (most hospitals won't let you leave without one)

- Crib or bassinet/ moses basket & mattress

- Go-bag and/or diaper bag (soon to be your new best friend as a new dad!)

The good news is that most of these items are items that "age out" for most families, which means that once their baby has grown up, they're often looking to sell or even give these items away. We may always have to invest in diapers/nappies, but it's nice to know there could be an easier way to get some of these bigger purchases.

If you know what other types of smaller items (or even big ones) you and your partner are looking for, it's a great idea to make a baby registry. Even if you don't have a baby shower in the works, the registry can help you plan what you need and even organize some budgeting numbers.

REFLECTIONS FROM OUR DADS

"Registries nowadays are so much easier than before. If you go on Amazon you can make one and continually add stuff over the course of the pregnancy. Then you just send a link to friends and family, and they can see whether or not an item has been purchased. We used that and Target, but Target had the added bonus of being able to scan things in store. As an added bonus, both shops gave us a little starter kit for our baby as a gift! Definitely worth looking into."
- David R. North Carolina, US.

"I can't tell you how helpful marketplaces, garage sales, family members, and goodwill has been for the pregnancy. Sometimes it really feels like it takes a village, and the village has been so immensely helpful to both of us."
— Kevin H. Utah, US.

"Somehow, it seems like I never thought I'd feel *ready* to have a kid. There was always something, financials, or the right time in life. The thing they don't tell you is all that stuff, you'll figure out. It seems like a lot, but broken down over time and over days and years, you'll figure it out."
— Jan T. Warsaw, Poland

"The gravity of the situation is slowly starting to sink in. On the financial side of things, I'm the only income earner in the house. I constantly question if this means I need to be locked into a job for the rest of my life? Also, because we're in a one bed apartment there's more stress to move."

- Fred S, London, UK.

"In our area there was a nonprofit called "Free to Be a Kid" where people would donate all their old clothes, and then once a month they would have a huge sale where you would pay five dollars and fit as many clothes into a garbage bag as you could—and baby clothes are tiny! We got three years worth of clothes for $10. You might want to encourage dads to look for similar nonprofits in their area!

- Keith G. Seattle, US.

☑ WEEKLY CHECKLIST

☐ Talk to your partner about potential baby names!

☐ Talk to your partner about the registry options and get it started:

    ☐ There are a variety of stores and many will offer gifts when you register with them.

    ☐ Some stores also offer the opportunity to walk through with a scanner to find exactly what you're looking for.

☐ Prepare your budget for some of the larger pregnancy expenses and check local community groups, non-profits, or donation groups for help!

☐ A few ideas and possible add-ons for the **baby registry:**

    ☐ Infant car-seat (they won't let you leave the hospital without one).

    ☐ Infant stroller.

    ☐ Crib & Mattress.

    ☐ Bassinet/moses basket & Sheets.

    ☐ Bibs & burp cloths.

    ☐ Diaper Genie (unless you're going down the re-usable diaper/nappy route exclusively).

    ☐ Baby bathtub.

    ☐ Baby bottles.

    ☐ Wearable dad harness/carrier to hold the baby (with good support!).

    ☐ Newborn clothes (make sure you prepare for the season, whether warm or cold, that your baby will be born into).

IN THE GROOVE

TERMS TO KNOW

Brown Fat – A special type of fat that keeps babies at the right temperature.

Subcutaneous Fat – The jiggly fat visible just under the skin, has been known to protect us from certain diseases.

Apocrine Glands – Sweat glands that activate during puberty and come with that oh so lovely body odor (B.O.).

Eccrine Glands – Sweat glands maintain good body temperature and are very active when working out.

MOTHER AND BABY

Now the size of a potato (5.1 inches & 5.9 ounces), your baby is working hard this week to put a little meat on those newly developing bones with the addition of "brown fat." They begin to form this layer of fat under the skin to help them better regulate their internal temperature.

Unlike regular fat in our bodies that is just there to store excess energy, "brown fat" actually helps produce heat to keep the baby warm. It also has a huge impact on metabolism as they are now *hungrier than ever.*

In addition to brown fat, your baby is building sweat glands—starting with the hands and feet and moving inwards. There are two types of sweat glands that develop: *eccrine glands* appear all over the body, but the baby won't activate them until a few weeks after birth. They're the glands that cool us down when we get too hot, which is why first-time parents put a big focus on baby's temperature—they can't sweat yet!

The other glands are called *apocrine glands*, and although the baby develops them right now at seventeen weeks, they won't be activated until puberty. The big difference between the two is that apocrine glands bring that wonderful B.O. when sweating. But that's still years and *years* away—plenty of time to stock up deodorant in the meantime!

The perfect way to round out month four is to know that the baby can finally hear you! That's right, the ears that started on the neck have moved into place, and even they won't necessarily recognize your voice just yet, as it still sounds more like a distant car horn when underwater—but they are definitely starting to.

Keep in mind, however, that the womb is an extremely loud place already. In addition to your voice and their mother's, your baby is going to hear the inner workings of your partner's body from stomach digestion even down to her blood flow. With that in mind, in planning for the future, don't worry if you live next to a busy road or an apartment with thin walls—babies aren't necessarily used to silence when sleeping or resting, and they'll adapt to just about any environment after birth because of that.

In terms of your partner, Week 17 often marks a welcome return of energy, sex drive, and even some appetite. (The smells that made her sick might even be returning to normal!) However, something important to note in Week 17 is healthy weight gain. It's nearly inevitable that your partner will be conscious of weight during their pregnancy. The amount of weight gain can vary depending on the size of your partner before pregnancy began. However, by Week 17, it's common to have gained 10 to 15 pounds (4.5 – 6.8 kg) with an additional one to two pounds each week during the second and third trimesters. Take these measures with a grain of salt, of course, as no two women will gain weight the same way during pregnancy.

Let's take a deeper look at this. If a woman gains thirty pounds (13.6 kg) from a pregnancy, that weight might break down like this:

Baby:	7.5 pounds (3.4 kg) - average size upon delivery
Placenta:	1.5 pounds (.7 kg)
Amniotic fluid/sac:	2 pounds (.9 kg)
Uterus:	2 pounds (.9 kg)
Breast tissue from pregnancy:	2 pounds (.9 kg)
Blood volume from pregnancy:	4 pounds (1.8 kg)
Fluids found in any maternal tissue:	4 pounds (1.8 kg)
Fat stores from pregnancy:	7 pounds (3.2 kg)

All said, pregnancy can account for a lot of added weight. The only time to be concerned is if there is especially fast weight gain, or if it's affecting your partner psychologically. A lot of women have a hard time coming to terms with how fast their body is changing, and they often need extra support and reassurance.

If that is something your partner experiences during the pregnancy, try to remind them that even though the perception of their body might be having a hard time catching up with its constantly changing shape on the **outside**, it can also offer a shift in focus—one that might help them turn that perception on its head, and appreciate what it represents—the constantly growing life on the **inside**.

WHAT'S HAPPENING WITH YOU - 'STORYTIME' WITH BABY

It can feel like there is a lot of time between ultrasounds and check-ups over the course of the pregnancy. During that time, it's easy to get overtaken by anxiety and worry if your baby is doing okay. As dads, we always want to make sure that they're getting everything they need or that they're moving enough in there.

But take this to heart: by Week 17, your baby can start to hear the sound of your voice. Sure, it'll sound muffled, but it's completely normal that the very first voices the baby will recognize will be yours and your partners. With that, it can be a nice bonding experience with both your partner and your baby to start telling stories to them. It can be 'storytime with dad,' or you can simply talk about your day while near your partner's belly, or maybe even play some music for them.

As exciting as it is to get constant updates about your baby's developmental progress over the course of the pregnancy, it's equally amazing to find moments to simply connect with them. There's no right or wrong way to talk to your baby—just *talk*.

The great benefit of communicating with your baby while they're still in the womb is that your voice can really soothe them, or even lull them to sleep. By the time they arrive and are suddenly experiencing a crazy amount of stimuli, your voice might be the thing that makes them feel safe, at home, and calms them down.

It really can be a special moment to experience.

REFLECTIONS FROM OUR DADS

"I ended up buying a little voice recorder for my wife to talk to my baby. I record and send messages, stories or just talking about my day, to her so that she can put headphones on her belly and allow our baby to hear my voice. It makes me feel that much closer, even when I'm away."
- Dean F. Kansas, US.

"I know my wife was pretty concerned about her weight gain, and to be honest, I was a little concerned with my sympathy weight. But eventually, she really did seem to settle into it, even become more confident because of it."
— Taylor W. Washington, US.

"Sometimes, I wondered when I rested my head on my partner's leg if it bothered her when I just started talking to our baby. We hadn't named him yet, but I just liked introducing myself and talking about nothing, really. It became a favorite pastime—I think for all of us."
— James G. California, US.

☑ WEEKLY CHECKLIST

☐ Start some of your very own baby 'storytime'!

☐ Make your very first "Baby Playlist" of your favorite music.

    ☐ In the coming weeks, you might even get a response of baby flutters or kicks to some great songs!

☐ Ask your doctor about the *Quad Screen* – another genetic blood test that measures the levels of four substances produced by the fetus and the placenta to check for any potential abnormalities.

CHAPTER FIVE

MONTH FIVE

Month five is the halfway month! You are now officially halfway to meeting your beautiful baby. In addition to that amazing milestone, month five is really where your partner's baby bump starts to show. She might not be waddling around lifting all that "brown fat" that the baby is putting on, but she's almost definitely starting to show. It's a bit surreal to see—you knew the baby was in there, of course, but now you have this ever-present reminder, and that's a wonderful thing. Sometimes that can make our over-protective instincts come through—but hey, that's precious cargo in there!

Beyond just showing in month five, it also might be the first month your partner feels those first baby kicks (sometimes on her bladder at 3 a.m., triggering a rush to the bathroom), and the first time you might actually see those kicks too.

Finally, month five could be the big month of discovering the baby's birth gender! It's possible you already know from the genetic testing, or maybe you're waiting to find out—either way, this month, you're halfway there!

PREGNANCY PAINS & GENDER IDENTITIES

TERMS TO KNOW

Myelin (Sheath) – This thin membrane covers the nerves and helps brain signals in the fetus travel up to 100 times faster; super important for those big brain moves and neural development.

Edema – Excess fluid trapped in the body that can cause swelling, which tends to happen a lot in the feet!

4D Ultrasounds – A higher level of ultrasound that shows more 3D movement of your baby in the womb.

Varicose Veins – Twisted, enlarged veins commonly seen in pregnant women.

MOTHER AND BABY

Your baby bell pepper! (5.6 inches & 6.7 ounces.) This week marks the point where doctors should be able to determine the sex of your baby. Although cutting-edge 4D ultrasounds may be able to tell you as soon as fourteen weeks (sometimes sooner), most standard ultrasound technology will be able to identify the sex of your baby by the seventeen-eighteen week mark. Whether that impacts your decisions in planning for the baby, or if you even want to know the sex ahead of time, it is entirely up to you.

Besides the sex, two other big things are happening for the baby this week. For one, they're really honing in on their napping skills. Once your partner starts feeling those flutters or kicks, they might also notice when the baby is most active—or when they're most relaxed. Surprisingly, when your partner is active—walking or exercising or going about daily routines—that's usually when the baby is napping. The movement tends to lull them to sleep naturally.

On the other hand, when your partner is lying in bed or relaxing on the couch, there might be a sudden uptick in the baby's activity. As she prepares to relax, they yell, "rise and shine!" and start throwing their own little disco party in your partner's uterus. As mentioned by one of our dads, they especially love landing the pile-driver on mother's bladder at 3 a.m.

As far as your partner this week, hopefully she's starting to get a hold of the second trimester. Once the baby starts to move more, they will require a bit more energy, and they only have one place to get it from—your partner. With more blood going to the baby, your partner might be feeling even less energy for herself—and lower blood pressure can often mean a bit of added fatigue or drowsiness.

This might also be the first week your partner experiences some *edema* or swelling from fluid build-up (usually in the feet). It's often nothing to worry about, even if it can be annoying. Another instance of swelling this week might come from your partner's veins, which can swell up blue or purple above the skin from increased blood flow and circulation. These are called *varicose veins*, and to prevent them, your partner is encouraged to focus on maintaining healthy circulation.

One way to do that is by using an elliptical or exercise bike at the gym, but if either of those aren't available, going on walks together can work wonders by increasing calf muscle strength (a place where the veins appear most commonly).

Additionally, if you see your partner struggling with some tighter clothes this week or month, it might be a good time to surprise them with a cozy maternity outfit.

WHAT'S HAPPENING WITH YOU - ON GENDERS & IDENTITIES

Advancements in medical technology have allowed us to know more about our developing babies than ever before. Because of that, "gender reveal parties" have become all the rage. Only a few decades ago, most prospective parents waited until delivery to discover the gender of the baby—nowadays that is becoming rarer and rarer. A lot of parents discover their baby's gender right when doctors can determine it, and they celebrate that discovery with friends and family—and, sometimes, social media.

When you find out your baby's gender, it also might bring to mind some issues surrounding gender that are prevalent in our world today. You might not like the idea of gender reveal parties, or the attribution of gender identities. Or perhaps a gender reveal party is something you and your partner are excited to share as an experience with loved ones.

No matter your position, it's important to keep in mind that the decisions of how to raise your baby, and what values you'll teach them, are entirely up to you and your partner. You're going to be their caretakers, their protectors, their providers, and their parents. No one will be able to tell you exactly how you should raise your child, and even if they do, you'll find out pretty soon that nearly everyone has been winging it for all of human existence. No one will have all the answers, and we'll all make different mistakes and experience different successes. It's life, and for the time being, your values are the ones that will be shared with your child.

You'll be their first teacher of right and wrong, and their first guide to experience it. It's an awesome responsibility, but it's also not one to worry too much about. If you throw a gender reveal party with pink and blue, or if you throw one with ambivalent colors, or if you don't throw one at all—it's *your* choice to make.

As long as you're making your decisions out of love for your child-to-be and in celebration of the miracle of their life, you're doing alright. Be compassionate, be conscious, but also be confident of how you feel.

REFLECTIONS FROM OUR DADS

"My partner and I thought about not having a party at all.
We definitely didn't want to have the traditional blue/
pink gender reveal. We still wanted to celebrate, though,
so we had this nice party and cut open a cake to have
rainbow Skittles fall out rather than find out how our baby
is developing. Everybody had a good time, and to boot the
Skittles were the perfect accent to the cake!"
— Thomas H. Sydney, AUS.

"During COVID, it was
pretty nice to have our
own virtual gender
reveal. It ended up being
this huge Zoom call
with dozens of friends
and family, and they all
cheered and were having
a great time when we
set off these confetti
poppers. IT'S A GIRL!"
— James G. California, US.

"With my family in Germany and Amy's miles away in England it was definitely hard as it felt like we were going through the pregnancy alone. Not being able to share the experience with friends and family was tough, however, lockdown was a blessing in disguise as having to work from home meant we could spend a lot more time together."
- Matteo V. Surrey, UK.

"We went back for our scan this week and it didn't even fit in the whole picture. They had to keep moving it just to get a good image. It's amazing how fast it all goes."
- Fred S. London, UK.

☑ WEEKLY CHECKLIST

☐ Get ready and excited for the *20-Week Anatomy Scan*—another opportunity to see your baby and how they've grown already!

☐ Make a list of any odd jobs around the home you'd like to do in preparation for the baby.

☐ Talk with your partner about any potential baby announcement party!

SKIN DEFENSE & HAIRLINES

TERMS TO KNOW

Round-Ligament Pain – Muscles stretching to accommodate the baby can cause sharp pain in your partner's abdomen and side.

Vernix Caseosa – A thick, slime-like, greasy substance that coats the baby to protect them from scratching themselves.

Anatomy Ultrasound – Level 2 ultrasound to determine gender and measurements of the baby.

MOTHER AND BABY

In Week 19, your baby is now the ultimate power fruit: a mango (6 inches & 8.5 ounces)! They've grown a ton in the last few weeks, and your partner's uterus is no doubt feeling the stretch, usually with cramping and the start-up of some round ligament pain, which we'll go into in a bit.

What's exciting this week is how your baby is adapting to protect themselves during development. Seriously, this whole cycle works like a well-oiled machine—and yet, both the baby and your partner are completely new to it. That's crazy! Your partner might have never grown a baby before, and your baby has certainly never grown before—but here we are, a process that couldn't be more efficient if you planned each part down to the molecule.

This week, your baby is developing *vernix caseosa*. We already mentioned the hair-like lanugo a few weeks ago, but the vernix is a thick, almost slime-like substance that coats baby and protects them from drying out—and also from their brand-new fingernails. Talk about perfect design; it shows up right when the baby has fingernails that they *could* scratch themselves with.

Additionally, your baby has a fresh hairline starting this week. The scalp hair has moved through the hair tunnel or canal (the uppermost part of a hair follicle) and is now setting in place to grow on the baby's head. There's one old wives' tale that still holds up today to scientific scrutiny: *If a baby has a lot of hair, it can make the mother feel more heartburn.* The reason has less to do with the hair, however, and more to do with the hormones, much like similar pregnancy symptoms. As it turns out, significant increases in pregnancy hormones like estrogen and progesterone can relax muscles in the mother's stomach (esophageal sphincter), which can allow stomach acid back up into the esophagus to cause heartburn. It just so happens that the same mixture of hormones is linked to stimulating fetal hair growth.

In other words, more hair = more heartburn.

As for some potential challenges your partner may be facing, we have to talk about *round-ligament pain.* Yikes! It's the stretching of ligaments along the sides of the uterus, and it usually comes from standing too quickly, coughing, laughing, and very often, sneezing. While it isn't harmful to the baby, it hurts like a . . . well . . . *a mother.* This pain can vary in severity, usually coursing through the abdomen (often on the lower-right side), and it definitely can become a frequent nuisance for your partner. Doing some stretching and making slower movements can lessen the intensity of the round-ligament pain, but that doesn't always make it go away completely. If it's pervasive and not going away, contact your doctor.

Another common symptom this week is dizziness. Because of the baby's continued growth, the uterus is putting quite a bit of pressure on your partner's blood vessels, and the baby might be putting even more pressure on her lungs. Since the baby will continue to grow and expand, the best way to combat these symptoms is to drink enough water and eat a balanced diet because dehydration and lack of food can often make the feeling much worse.

WHAT'S HAPPENING WITH YOU - BABY MEASUREMENTS & STANDARDS

There's a bit of a theme when it comes to pregnancy and the first few years of life: your baby is constantly being pitted against the measures and standards of other babies. At the twenty-week anatomy scan (often next week), measurements are used to determine the pace at which your baby is developing. That can be amazingly helpful, but it can also be concerning because of the **inevitability of comparison.**

Every part of the pregnancy process is measured against standards set from a whole slew of statistics across a whole variety of situations—the trouble is, it's hard to know exactly where your baby fits within those statistics. In other words, we use these measurements to develop a framework so we can understand what's happening with our baby—**but your baby is still the one calling the shots.** They're growing at *their* pace. That might be faster, that might be slower. They might arrive at thirty-eight weeks or sooner—they might arrive exactly on their due date, or later.

Once they're born, they'll have certain milestones—rolling over, crawling, walking, talking. You'll hear about how their brain is developing in comparison to other babies, how their reflexes are attuning in comparison to others at the same age. Without being conscious of it, it can be overwhelming, exhausting, and unhealthy.

All we want to bring attention to is that these measurements and statistics are great for keeping track of how your baby is developing both physically and mentally, but too much information can also be a double-edged sword. We might get frantic that our baby is measuring crown to rump just below the average at twenty weeks, or that they aren't as vocal at six months. The key to remember is these averages help us understand most babies, but they aren't *our* babies.

With all that in mind, try not to let too much information add unneeded stress or color your impression of progress. Your baby is *your* baby, and as long as you and your partner are making the best choices you can, their pace of everything is the *right* pace.

REFLECTIONS FROM OUR DADS

"This was the ultrasound I was expecting from the beginning, the one from the movies with the gel on the belly and everything. But it was better, almost an hour of watching our baby. The craziest part, as we were waiting for the doctor to come explain the results, a fire caught on the lower level of the hospital and we were evacuated! We ended up getting the results rundown in the parking lot. Pretty memorable."
— David R. North Carolina, US.

"One of the coolest things about the scan was we thought we were only getting pictures, and then they sent us basically a GIF of our baby that looked like they were almost doing finger guns like the Fonz. That's my boy!"
— John C. California, US.

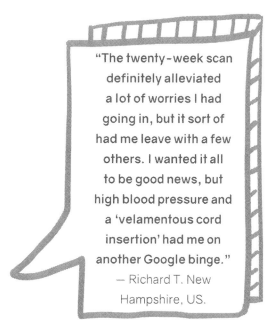

"The twenty-week scan definitely alleviated a lot of worries I had going in, but it sort of had me leave with a few others. I wanted it all to be good news, but high blood pressure and a 'velamentous cord insertion' had me on another Google binge."

— Richard T. New Hampshire, US.

☑ WEEKLY CHECKLIST

☐ Start thinking about the possibility of a daycare! It's never too early to start planning and a great many of them have a wait-list.

☐ Also look into nannies or sitters as another option!

☐ Keep in mind that the Maternal Serum Screening or Quad Screen Blood Test are typically done between 15 weeks and 22 weeks.

☐ Sign up for prenatal classes in your community—we'll talk more about them later, but sometimes they have specific dates set out so it's good to get a jump on it!

WEEK 20

HALFWAY THERE!

TERMS TO KNOW

Quickening – The feeling of the baby fluttering inside the mother's womb, very easy to mistake for gas.

Velamentous Cord Insertion – A rare pregnancy complication where the umbilical cord inserts on the side of the placenta.

Marginal Cord Insertion – A pregnancy condition where the cord inserts just off of the center of the placenta.

Meconium – Dark green and tar-like, it's the first feces of the newborn baby.

MOTHER AND BABY

Ba-boom! Your baby is officially a banana! (6.5 inches & 10.2 ounces.) More than that, you are officially halfway through the forty weeks of pregnancy! Week 20 is a huge milestone, and the baby is working hard to practice their breathing, swallowing, and even a few somersaults. Odds are that your partner might be feeling more and more flutters, also called *quickening*, although many mothers say it's easy to confuse with gas bubbling around inside.

At Week 20, the baby's brain and ears are working in tandem. Their face is nearly fully developed, and this is often the week that you go in for your anatomy screening! There's nothing better than getting an update on the baby's development and getting some new pics to boot!

As for your partner, Week 20 is often one where many women feel another uptick in energy—even if they also might experience shortness of breath after those sudden bursts of energy. A lot of doctors might recommend that your partner start eating bananas (perfect timing!) or potassium filled-foods or supplements, as leg cramps can become common when the baby banana themselves start consuming potassium stores. Doctors also will recommend water for the cramping, but surprisingly, with the baby putting so much pressure on your partner's digestive system, even certain types of water have been known to cause heartburn and acid reflux in pregnant women.

It sounds odd, but pure water typically has a PH (*potential of hydrogen*, used to measure acidity) of 7, or neutral. However, drinking water with other foods could raise the acidity of those foods, causing some acid reflux. Additionally, other types of water like flavored or mineral can disrupt the mineral balance in a pregnant woman's body also causing those symptoms. To add, too much water can also cause the stomach to distend (swell), which is already being impacted by the growing fetus, and that acid might be pushing back up the esophagus as a result to cause heartburn. It sounds like a lot, but all that still doesn't make water any less vital. As always, it's all about testing out which foods or drinks work and which don't.

With the anatomy scan in or around this week, seeing your baby in such detail can really help you keep things in perspective. Twenty weeks down, twenty to go!

WHAT'S HAPPENING WITH YOU - THE ANATOMY ULTRASOUND

It's become standard practice for expectant mothers to receive a Level 2 Ultrasound in the second trimester somewhere between eighteen and twenty-two weeks, though the most common tends to be twenty weeks—giving it the nickname the *20-Week Anatomy Scan*. This is a full-body scan of the baby and one of the most in-depth looks you will get before birth.

The scan itself can take forty-five minutes to an hour (sometimes longer), and that's not counting the time waiting for the ultrasound technician to analyze all the measurements or for the doctor to come in and explain the findings. Even though your partner doesn't need to do anything diet-wise for this particular scan (other than drinking a good amount of water), it's best to have a meal beforehand because you'll be at the appointment for a bit!

Beyond the time it takes, this scan is really exciting. Not only will you see your baby in the most detail you ever have (and they've likely developed a lot from last time), but you'll also get answers as to *how* they are developing.

The scan will measure (and take pictures or short videos) of the baby's face, brain, spine, heart, kidneys, diaphragm, chest, stomach, bladder, arms, legs, feet, hands, umbilical cord, as well as the genitals. The technician will also measure the full size of the fetus to estimate gestational age, alongside the placenta and amniotic fluid to see if there are any potential complications.

All said, this scan gives the full rundown of your baby. The best part about it is that you no longer feel "in the dark." The doctor will take all the information and explain it to you in detail, setting your mind at ease from all the various complications you might have been imagining. This will help you refine your focus as you move towards the third trimester. To add, these are going to be the best pictures you have of the baby so far, and seeing how they're interacting with the world around them—how much they've grown—is a very special part of the pregnancy.

REFLECTIONS FROM OUR DADS

"I sometimes get a bit obsessed with data, always analytical. So, each week of the pregnancy, I was tracking every average measurement and symptom I could. I thought it was helping me, but I realized it was almost keeping me in this constant state of anxiety. Not only about my baby right now, but about its future."
— Richard T. New Hampshire, US.

"It's honestly a bit wild how much they can tell you about your baby, and as early as they can tell it. As it goes, we really love all the updates, but more than that, we just love getting new pictures to post on the fridge with our little calendar countdown."
— Thomas A. Nebraska, US.

"Seeing my partner's body change and her belly starting to pop out was such a great high for me during the pregnancy."
- Royce B. California, US.

☑ WEEKLY CHECKLIST

☐ Celebrate the halfway point of the pregnancy by going out and seeing friends or having a cozy night in with a good film!

☐ Ask your doctors about the Glucose and Gestational Diabetes Test.

☐ Schedule the 24-week prenatal visit.

☐ If you both want one, talk about the possibility of a baby shower and where it might be fun to have it. Not all of them are exclusive to women (some double as family or friend reunions!).

WEEK
21

THE TRAIN KEEPS ROLLING

TERMS TO KNOW

Hemoglobin – Proteins that carry oxygen to make red blood cells.

Myoglobin – Proteins that carry oxygen to make muscle cells.

Iron – Pregnant women need double the amount of iron to make both of the above proteins.

Nesting – A natural urge many pregnant women have to clean and organize their home in preparation for the baby.

MOTHER AND BABY

We hope you celebrated the halfway point because now we're pushing forward to the birth. Your baby for sure didn't slow down, not even for a minute! They are now the size of a big carrot (10.5 inches & 12.7 ounces) and, like Bugs Bunny, they are practicing bouncing around in there. Well, Bugs isn't the most active bunny, but your baby sure is.

Week 21 often comes with a pretty significant uptick in activity with the baby. Quite literally, they start rocking and rolling in there— rolling with constant somersaults and, as far as rocking, this is the time in pregnancy where a lot of people start playing classical music for their baby (like Bach, Chopin, Mozart, or Beethoven) to help stimulate their brain waves and "make them smarter."

That last part is a bit of misappropriated conventional wisdom. In reality, playing music teaches your baby, like anything else, *familiarity*. This means that if you play a song to them in the womb enough, they'll likely recognize it outside the womb. The benefit is that babies often experience sensory overload outside of the womb, and the music they heard while inside can sometimes soothe them—they'll feel *at home* once more. The other added benefit is that making a "Baby Playlist" or just singing to your baby can be a great way to relax and connect with your partner.

On the developmental side, your baby is now using iron to make red blood cells and muscle cells—both of which contain oxygen-carrying proteins called hemoglobin and myoglobin, respectively. This process happens in the spleen and liver at first, but now bone marrow is hopping into the mix. The importance? Oxygenation and muscle building make the baby strong! On the flip side, your baby is appropriating all that iron from your partner. If she is feeling overly tired or short of breath, her iron stores might be low. Spinach, raspberries, whole-wheat bread, and raisins all have a good bit of iron, so try recommending those if she asks. If the symptoms seem pervasive, always talk to your healthcare provider for some added help.

At Week 21, your partner might also be experiencing some new symptoms. At this point, her milk ducts are fully developed and prepared for the baby—and they might start leaking a little. If it happens out in public, be sure to bring some extra shirts, nipple pads, or have a jacket you can lend her should the situation arise.

Additionally, because of the sudden weight gain that often happens in pregnancy, many women will start to see stretch marks develop on their bellies which can also dry out the skin. Although these aren't likely to dissipate until after the birth, you can get some belly butter or pregnancy-safe body oils to lessen the symptoms. If the dry skin turns itchy, it could be a rare but annoying pregnancy condition called a PUPPP skin rash: *Pruritic Urticarial Papules and Plaques of Pregnancy*. Sheesh, even the name is annoying!

WHAT'S HAPPENING WITH YOU - NESTING AND A DWINDLING NEST-EGG

Around the time of the anatomy scan and just after, you might start to notice some habit changes with your partner. The changes might involve a little more tidying around the home, some deep cleaning, some intense organizing, some new home projects, or a slew of packages that arrive suddenly outside the door. *ANOTHER ONE?!?!*

Welcome to *nesting*.

Although nesting is extremely common a few weeks before the baby arrives, it can begin for some women at any time during pregnancy. Some women never experience the nesting instinct, but the reason we bring it up now is because you might be in the early stages of nesting around the second trimester. The word can function as a catch-all for *preparing the home for the baby*, and in that sense, nesting can also include some new financial investments.

That said, early nesting can be helpful. In a lot of ways, early nesting habits can help you plan for some proactive action. For example, if you and your partner plan to have a nursery for the baby (not everyone does), getting it started as soon as possible can be a real help for both of you for a couple of reasons.

For one, your partner at this stage likely isn't as fatigued as she might be in the third trimester, so you can get some much-appreciated assistance. And two, the longer you wait, the more frantic the nesting just before delivery can be.

The more small-scale projects you can get done over a long period of time, the less they'll become monstrous projects later on—when you already have plenty more to think about. Not to mention, some of the biggest costs in a pregnancy come from the delivery and hospital stay, so it can be a big relief to spread other payments out well before that.

REFLECTIONS FROM OUR DADS

"It's really interesting what your baby responds to. Sometimes we'll play a song and my partner says they start to kick. You wonder if they're like, 'turn that music off, it's horrible!' Or they're dancing around in there. We always imagine the latter."
— Emmanuel V. Texas, US.

"That was the shift I was ready for and didn't think I was capable of when it came to finances or any life decision really. But all the things we as dads take care of behind the scenes, everything I do, I'm thinking of them. My family."
- Barrett E. Chicago, US.

"I decided I HAD to remodel our garage two weeks before the baby arrived. Yes, I needed to create a new office space to make room for the nursery, but did I have to wait until right up until the end? Definitely not!"

- Keith G. Seattle, US.

☑ WEEKLY CHECKLIST

☐ Think about maternity pictures as a possible gift for your partner—it's an opportunity to photograph her and her new "bump" with the baby. You could even join in and make it an outing!

☐ Talk with your partner about daycare, a sitter, a nanny, or how childcare might look for you both.

☐ Look for the signs of early nesting and see if there are any projects you can knock out ahead of time!

A POUND, SHYLOCK!

TERMS TO KNOW

Braxton Hicks Contractions – Random, intermittent feeling of muscles squeezing across the belly that foreshadow real contractions during labor. Also called "false labor" pains, they tend to last about thirty seconds.

MOTHER AND BABY

Holy moly, your baby is now a whole *pound* (.45 kg) and flaunting it! They are the size of a coconut (10.2 inches & 15.2 ounces), and they're moving, grooving, and ready to party. At Week 22, they also have a fully formed face and are practicing squinting and

smiling in every way they possibly can. As mentioned, their hearing is only getting better from here on out, so now they can listen in on muffled music, big-screen movies, and maybe even your partner singing in the shower. More than that, their eyes are now sensitive to light, meaning they might actually turn away if she lays out in the sun or you shine a phone light in search of a potential kick.

This week your baby is also developing their tear ducts. Although the baby can't cry tears for up to four weeks after birth, the tear ducts are formed and preparing for well . . . *a likely* good bit of use later. And, finally, this is the week where your baby's lovely heartbeat can be heard with a stethoscope (or even a fun phone app). Their heartbeat is still *thump-thump-thumping* away at around 110-160 bpm, compared to yours or your partner's, which usually sit somewhere around 60-100 bpm.

And speaking of your partner, this week (though it can be as early as Week 20), she could be feeling the famous *Braxton Hicks contractions*. They are the tightening of the muscles in the uterus that can make the belly feel hard to the touch. They are often irregular, and not all mothers feel them severely, but they essentially function as "practice contractions"—the way their body prepares for the real thing during labor. They usually dissipate as any cramp does, but before that, they can really take your partner's breath away.

In addition to your partner's new nemesis, Braxton Hicks, she might also be experiencing some other changes this week in the form of increased vaginal discharge, a newly "outie" belly button, and potential backaches. There's not much to do about the first two; the belly button just means the baby is getting cozy and growing, and vaginal discharge is par for the course—though it can feel strange when there's more than normal. As always, the only thing to be concerned about is if it's yellow, greenish, or has a pungent odor.

As for the last, if your partner is experiencing backaches, think about investing in a heating pad, pregnancy pillow, or prenatal massage. Try whatever helps ease the pain because, unfortunately, as the baby keeps growing, it might become more common.

WHAT'S HAPPENING WITH YOU - THINKING ABOUT PATERNITY LEAVE

By now, it's likely that quite a few people, if not everyone, knows that your partner is pregnant. In the coming weeks, with the baby bump becoming more and more pronounced, it becomes almost impossible to keep it quiet any longer. That said, your employers *might* know about the baby and the due date, but right now, if you haven't already, it's a good time to think about what kind of leave you'd like to take—and what's available to you.

Many jobs offer paternity leave of up to two weeks—but depending on your job and where you live, it's hard to say whether they'll pay you for those two weeks, or offer you something different. Either way, try to create an open dialogue with your employer and make sure they're in the loop for what you're planning—or hoping to receive. No one typically reacts well to things sprung upon them last-minute, so the sooner you have the conversation, the more time you have to get your ducks in a row before delivery.

The nuances of paternity leave can be tough to navigate with every job, and so whatever paternity leave you're allowed to have, try your best to take at least two weeks where you can focus on your baby, your partner, and yourself. If you can afford to take more time, that can be amazing—and totally worth it. However, you also might be ready to get back to work by then. It's hard to guess your situation, but those two weeks can be extremely vital to settle into a new life routine.

Paternity leave in many organizations is still playing catch up to what a whole new generation of dads really want, and if you find yourself in that culture, remember to have confidence that the time you take is well-deserved. There's a lot going on in your head, and you'll have a whole new set of responsibilities. Trying to balance all of them at once without the opportunity to separate them first can overwhelm just about anyone.

REFLECTIONS FROM OUR DADS

"This was actually one of the first weeks I saw our baby moving from the outside. The kick was so small, but that's all it was, a little push outward on the belly. I think I sat there for ten minutes after just waiting to see it again."
— Kyle P. Texas, US.

"Because we were having Twins — we had a scan every 4 weeks. I always got nervous a few days before a scan. Then I would feel really relieved during it."
- Adam I. London, UK.

"My wife literally curses at Braxton Hicks sometimes. I'll be in the other room and I'll hear her yell, 'F$#@ you, Brax!!' It seems annoyingly painful, but it's a little funny too."
— Emmanuel V. Texas, US

☑ WEEKLY CHECKLIST

☐ If you haven't already decided on a baby name, keep talking with your partner about it. You never know when inspiration might strike!

☐ Make sure you have the *Glucose Screening for Gestational Diabetes* appointment in the calendar.

☐ If you haven't already, start talks with your employer or anyone you need to about a plan for paternity leave.

CHAPTER SIX

MONTH SIX

The final month of the second trimester! Time can fly or stand still, and by now, you've surely felt both. Your partner is looking the part of a lovely pregnant woman, and this is the month she might see the full-on transition to maternity clothes (as we've heard, they are *super* comfy).

Other than the visible changes, she also might be feeling a good bit of heartburn, hot flashes, backaches, and Braxton Hicks. The reason for all these symptoms is exactly what you'd expect: a larger and more active baby is living it up on the inside. Your baby now has a full set of fingerprints, growing lungs, and a penchant for play. They are kicking, jabbing, squeezing, swallowing, and peeing to their little heart's content. And that's *a lot*. Fortunately, they can't make too much of an impact given their tiny size, but they can definitely startle your partner. She might wake up at night or get a sudden jolt on the couch—but it's all in good fun and usually, a welcome reminder of the excitement of the delivery day fast approaching.

As for you, this is the *last month* of the second trimester! That means anything that's been on the back-burner of your to-do list might need to get bumped up. We're almost two-thirds of the way there, one third to go! You've got this!

23

INFLATE THE BALLOON!

TERMS TO KNOW

Bronchioles – Branches of the lungs where breathing happens.

Alveoli – Tiny air sacs at the end of the bronchioles where carbon dioxide is exchanged with oxygen.

Surfactant – Liquid that makes it possible for babies to breathe air after delivery.

MOTHER AND BABY

It's Week 23, and your baby is the size of a grapefruit! (11.4 inches & 1.2 pounds/.5 kg) All of the baby's major organs are well developed now, even if they might not be fully formed yet. Either way, the groundwork has been laid and *all systems are a go.* This week, the brain gets lots of new activity with fresh synapses firing—the baby is listening to everything outside and wondering what all that racket is!

That's all on the inside; on the outside, the baby's fingernails have now reached the ends of their fingers (and just a head's up, baby fingernails can get long *fast*, so try to invest in a good baby fingernail clipper set). The wrinkly skin that covers the baby is finally starting to fill out, which means they're absorbing as much nutrition from your partner as they possibly can. Everything your partner eats—from spicy to sour, from hot to cold—the baby is tasting it and extracting nutrition from it. They might even react with an extra little flutter to the meals they seem to enjoy!

As mentioned in previous weeks, the baby is swallowing a lot of amniotic fluid (rife with electrolytes, so it's pretty much their own natural version of *Gatorade or Powerade*), and that process is building up their lungs. Blood vessels are also continuing to develop so that they are ready to breathe outside air, and those *respiratory bronchioles* (lung airway branches) are taking root. Quite literally, the bronchioles of the lung actually look a lot like tree branches, and the leaves at the ends of those tree branches, the *alveoli* (tiny air sacs), are also forming.

With all that going on with the baby, your partner also might be experiencing a strange trade-off this week. As the baby's eyes are developing and becoming sensitive to light, your partner's eyes might actually feel like they are getting dry and her vision blurry. However, it really is just a coincidence that they sometimes happen at the same time. The baby's eyes represent development on a typical timeline, but your partner's eyes getting dry is often a result of more hormonal fluctuations or dehydration from continued morning sickness.

Other than that, the Braxton Hicks contractions and backaches might become more prominent this week. For Braxton Hicks, doctors recommend drinking plenty of water—though that advice probably won't go over well while she's having a contraction and cursing Mr. Hicks. They can be annoying, and breathtaking in a bad way, but as long as they go away relatively quickly (less than 30 seconds), they're an unfortunate par for the course. True labor contractions are often between 30 and 90 seconds and can become longer and more consistent over time.

Your partner might also be experiencing some more swelling in their ankles or feet this week. Since it's a build-up of fluid, the best way to help is to encourage your partner to kick back and put her feet up to reduce the swelling.

WHAT'S HAPPENING WITH YOU - THE CATCH-22 OF PREGNANCY DIETS

Over the course of the pregnancy, you might experience quite a few changes in your partner's cravings and food choices. Some things that might have been repulsive to her in the first trimester, she might be clambering for in the second trimester. Sometimes her appetite can go from non-existent to what some mothers refer to as a "black hole stomach." In that way, there's a Catch-22 to the pregnancy diet that you should look out for:

The healthiest thing for your partner might also make them sick.

We'd like to think that our bodies know instinctively what we *need* to eat. And sometimes, it seems that they do. If we don't drink water for a long enough time, we start to crave it (even smell it if we're dehydrated enough). If we've eaten too much junk food, we might feel sluggish or exhausted (even if we still want more). Unfortunately, even if your pregnant partner wants, say, a green smoothie—or *wants to want* a green smoothie—it's also entirely possible that they can't keep it down. It could cause acid reflux, heartburn, or they just can't bring themselves to drink it.

What do you do?

Obviously, you're in a position where you want to encourage them to eat something healthy for the baby, and you know that they *want* to. But you also see that they just can't handle eating it. If you try to force things, one way or the other, it is bound to be an un-winnable argument that only stresses you both out.

When it comes down to it, some food is often better than none. And what's more, severe or prolonged stress is more harmful to the baby's development than any food choice. The best thing you can do to help both your partner and the baby is to take each meal as *individual situations*. In some, you'll find the right solution. In others, you might not. As long as you and your partner are doing your best to make the right decisions, and showing *solidarity* in them, that's enough.

REFLECTIONS FROM OUR DADS

"I felt like there was a lot of unknown. It was super scary, especially in expressing my true self and how I felt. A lot of it was me juggling my own panic and stress. I tried to hide it, because I tried to be 'strong' and it feels selfish to express any types of feelings. I had my dad to talk to who said you just gotta figure it out as it comes."
    - Royce B. California, US.

"My wife was on her feet all day—she works retail—and by the end of those days, they were just so swollen she could hardly walk. It took time, but we were able to help her start her leave early. Thank goodness, we know not everyone gets that lucky."
    — Thomas M. Florida, US.

"I quit smoking for the duration of the pregnancy alongside my wife. And I didn't smoke again, other than socially. It's hard though. Men face expectations, I was battling another sickness at the time. I know you're supposed to make sure the kid is okay, and if you're dead you just can't do that. In my head, it was as simple as that."
    - Lee H. South Carolina, US

☑ WEEKLY CHECKLIST

☐ Make sure everything with your insurance is ready to go, and you know the upcoming costs.

☐ See if you can feel those first baby kicks!

☐ Talk with your partner about nursery designs if you plan to have one!

WEEK

24

HOUSTON, WE HAVE VIABILITY

TERMS TO KNOW

Gestational Diabetes – A condition where the mother's blood sugar becomes high during pregnancy and can be very dangerous for the baby if left untreated.

Linea Nigra – Dark vertical line that runs down from mother's belly button—also called the "pregnancy line."

MOTHER AND BABY

Your baby is the size of a pomegranate! (11.8 inches & 1.4 pounds/.6 kg). It really is a testament to how far we've come with medical and scientific advancements because Week 24 is considered the *week of viability*. That means that if the baby happens to be born prematurely, they have

enough of the basic foundation to survive outside the womb—so much so that babies born at 24 weeks have a 50-75% chance of going home with their families!

That simple fact can be a real relief, even if we always hope for a full-term pregnancy. And to prepare for that full-term, your baby is continuing to pack on the pounds. They are absorbing everything they can to build fat, all while kicking and punching in a non-stop in-womb workout to build muscle. The work is paying off—they put on almost 4 to 6 ounces each week from here on out! Talk about gains!

At the same time, your partner is probably also experiencing some continued weight gain from the pregnancy. From the beginning of the first trimester to now, most women have put on somewhere around fifteen pounds. After that, it's often an average of one to two pounds per week until delivery. Their breasts have also increased in size, along with their areolas, which quite literally become a bigger target for the baby to latch on to when and if breastfeeding comes around.

By now, doctors can easily guess the gestational age by measuring the pubic bone to the highest point of the uterus (just above the belly button). Another change to the belly this week is that some women might start to see linea nigra develop—a *small line* of darkened skin from the belly button (or slightly above) to the pubic bone. The line is completely harmless, but it's caused by pregnancy hormones and often won't fade until a few weeks after birth.

WHAT'S HAPPENING WITH YOU - GLUCOSE & GESTATIONAL DIABETES

Between Week 24 and Week 28, your doctor will likely order a *Glucose Challenge Screening Test*. This is a test to see if your partner has developed gestational diabetes by measuring how her body is processing sugar. To do that, doctors will have her drink a cup of sweet liquid called glucola and then draw blood an hour later to see how her body processed the sugar.

Before we get into what gestational diabetes means moving forward, you should be aware of three things. First, this is one of the longer doctor appointments, so make sure you plan to be there for over an hour. Second, some doctors encourage pregnant women not to eat many carbs or anything sugary before the test, as that's likely to make the results come up abnormal. Third, if the test comes up with results that worry the doctors, they'll order a different test, *the Glucose Tolerance Test*, which actually defines if your partner has gestational diabetes.

To make sure you're aware, in the UK and other places outside the US, doctors will often elect to go straight for the 3-hour glucose test rather than start with the screening. It's also possible that the hospital closest to you will follow that same guideline.

If your partner has gestational diabetes, *don't worry*. It isn't the end of the world. Gestational diabetes has become a much more common pregnancy condition than it has been in years prior. It occurs in 2 to 10% of pregnancies and, assuming your partner doesn't already have some form of diabetes, it only lasts for the duration of the pregnancy. The important thing is to take the test at the proper time so that gestational diabetes can be monitored more frequently—if it's left unchecked, that's when it becomes a problem.

There's really no agreed-upon cause of gestational diabetes other than the fact that hormones play a role. Doctors are aware of situations that put pregnant women at higher risk for gestational diabetes, such as having high blood pressure, a family history of diabetes, or being overweight—but none of those are considered direct causes.

If your partner is diagnosed with gestational diabetes, the treatment plan will depend on blood sugar levels measured throughout the day. An A1 plan (as it's often called) means that it can be controlled through diet alone, while an A2 plan means that insulin or oral medications might be required to keep blood sugar in check. Either way, it's important to get gestational diabetes under control as soon as possible because it increases the risk of pre-term birth and other complications—but if monitored and acted on properly, it's completely treatable.

REFLECTIONS FROM OUR DADS

"My wife is a Type 1 diabetic and her fear in all of our pregnancies is what many who encounter gestational diabetes come to fear: pre-term birth and complications. Fortunately, as long as you're diligent about nutrition and monitoring blood sugar, as she had become amazing at over all her years with Type 1, it can be kept under control."
— Noah A. Texas, US.

Gestational diabetes was a huge concern for us with my wife's prior health conditions. Luckily with supplements and management, it never showed up. Even if it had, as we became aware of the condition, we became equally aware of the treatments and that lessened the stress."
- Lee H. South Carolina, US.

☑ WEEKLY CHECKLIST

☐ Your prenatal appointment that often includes the Glucose Screening Test.

☐ Ask your doctor about *preeclampsia* and its symptoms.

☐ Schedule your next prenatal appointment.

☐ Talk to your partner about whether a *doula* would work for your birth —although they don't have medical training like a midwife or OB-GYN, they are there to help support your partner emotionally and can even help with post-partum care.

PRACTICE BREATHS & HICCUPS

TERMS TO KNOW

Pre-term birth (otherwise known as premature birth) – Babies born before 37 weeks.

High Blood Pressure – The force of blood flowing through your veins is higher than accepted averages (a.k.a. hypertension).

Preeclampsia – Pregnancy condition defined mostly by high blood pressure, protein in urine, and swelling.

NICU – Neonatal Intensive Care Unit, a place that cares for premature babies.

Hemorrhoids – A swollen vein or group of veins near the anus.

MOTHER AND BABY

At twenty-five weeks, your baby is as long as a whole cob of corn (13.6 inches & 1.5 pounds/.7 kg)! And with that length, your baby's objective this week: pack on the fat to fill out that long frame of bones and skin that's now becoming opaque (less translucent).

This week, your partner is probably starting to feel some *hiccups* coming from the baby. As the lungs are developing, and those alveoli (small sacs of air) at the end of the bronchioles (branches) are growing, your baby is taking a few practice "breaths." Seeing as how the baby has never done that before, they'll often take in a bit too much "air" and give themselves cute little hiccups. They also have a newfound sense of smell, which means when they "breathe" in, they're getting a hint of their first scent: amniotic fluid. And that's all made more adorable by the fact that they're also gaining far more brown fat to make them a cute little chunky-butt-hiccupping-flipping-baby in there.

Week 25 is also a refining time for the baby's reproductive system. If they're developing as a girl, those millions of eggs we talked about earlier have nearly reached their maximum amount. If they're developing as a boy, they have testes making the trek down to a still-developing scrotum.

As far as your partner this week, their weight is continuing to creep up, which may be affecting them psychologically. Seeing those changes happen so quickly can affect women in different ways. If you've been noticing your partner frowning in the mirror, do whatever you can to reassure her.

More than just weight, your partner might still be experiencing Braxton Hicks or trouble sleeping, but also some new symptoms in the form of extra-frequent urination and constipation. The baby putting all that added pressure on the bladder will likely continue to make bathroom breaks even more constant, but adding some walking activity or eating some fiber-rich foods like almonds (even light popcorn) can help with the constipation.

Finally, one very unfortunate cousin to varicose veins are varicose anal veins, or hemorrhoids. The added pressure that the baby is putting on your partner's digestive tract can cause *hemorrhoids*, and the best way to help is again, fiber-rich foods for constipation and also looking for pregnancy-safe topical treatments recommended by your doctor.

WHAT'S HAPPENING WITH YOU - PREMATURE POSSIBILITIES

As we move past the week of viability, the next thing we often think and worry about is the possibility of a premature delivery. The breakdown of carrying a baby to "term" has actually changed in the past few years. It used to be anywhere from 37 to 42 weeks, but now the division is a little more specific:

Pre-term / Premature	before 37 weeks
Early-term	37 weeks to 38 weeks and 6 days
Full-term	39 weeks to 40 weeks and 6 days
Late-term	41 weeks to 41 weeks and 6 days
Post-term	after 42 weeks

As mentioned, a premature baby is delivered any time before 37 weeks. There are also levels of pre-term babies that range from "extreme" at 25 weeks to "late" at 36 weeks, but by this point in the pregnancy, a premature baby is now *viable*. The more time they get in the womb, the higher their viability becomes. With each week, it ticks up a few more percentage points—which means they are likely to survive outside the womb because all the necessary components of life have been developed. However, even though a pre-term baby is viable, they are also at a much higher risk of complications simply because they didn't have enough time to finalize development in the womb.

Many things can increase the risk of pre-term labor, but very few of them are actually the root cause of it. Things like smoking, high blood pressure (hypertension), injury, or a stressful life event have all been known to contribute to pre-term labor—but the important thing to know is that if your baby is born pre-term, every week closer to their due date means there is less and less chance of complications.

If a baby is born pre-term, it's very likely they'll be taken to the NICU (Neonatal Intensive Care Unit) to receive treatment that can range anywhere from being placed in an incubator (artificial womb) to simply monitoring the baby's vital signs. Fortunately, with all the advancements in medical technology and the NICU in recent years, the chances of babies born pre-term going home with their parents healthy and normal are also increasing every year.

REFLECTIONS FROM OUR DADS

"It's strange, you get right over the hump of being afraid of miscarriages, but then you're right into the next stage of fear for a premature birth. I was big on data so after finding out about viability at Week 24 I was keeping a little measure to myself as each week the odds of a successful birth increased. This isn't something I recommend as it might just bring about more anxiety, but hard numbers have always helped me with stressors."
        - Richard T. New Hampshire, US.

"Our baby has always been crazy tall but really skinny, and it's been so important for us to not get caught up on the percentiles about weight gain and all that. He's growing at the right pace for him."
        - Keith G. Seattle, US.

"Just be there for your partner. She just needs all the help she can get at this stage, and she may be hiding feelings from you she may not be ready to discuss."
        - Jason O'C. Sydney, AUS.

☑ WEEKLY CHECKLIST

☐ Start speaking seriously with your partner about a birth plan—we'll go over it in more detail in Week 33 (we even have a sample version).

    ☐ *Where would you like to have the baby?*

        ☐ *Hospital, birthing center, home, etc.*

    ☐ *What are things that are important to you during the birth?*

    ☐ *Do you have any worries in regards to the birth?*

OPEN YOUR EYES

TERMS TO KNOW

Startle (Moro) Reflex – A reflex where infants think they're in a dangerous location and stretch out arms and legs, then cradle and cry for help.

Enzymes – Catalyst of chemical reactions in the body; anything from healing, growth, blood coagulation (scabbing), breathing, reproduction, digestion, and many others.

Stretch Marks – Irregular lines or streaks on the skin where it has been stretched, common in pregnancy.

MOTHER AND BABY

It's Week 26, and your baby is as big as a bunch of kale (14 inches and 1.7 pounds/.8 kg)! Really, really big, heavy kale. This week is often one of the most amazing weeks for the baby as they finally open their eyes for the first time! That's right, the sealed-shut eyelids have now developed enough to open, and your baby can see the world (sort of).

More than just fully formed eyes, they've got little eyelashes and eyebrows to adorn those beautiful pupils and irises. This development also might contribute to their reflexes being cranked up a notch this week. The *startle or moro reflex* is an instinctive reaction to stimuli, and you'll see it for yourself when they're born. Basically, if a baby thinks they're about to fall, they'll reach out their legs and arms or cradle close to lessen the impact of the fall—they might even cry out for you to protect them! It's remarkable what instincts babies have for survival right out of the womb—but more on that later.

It's definitely no fun to say this week brings yet another symptom your partner might experience, but we've said it before and we'll say it again: *making a baby is hard work!* It's a full-time job, and the latest symptoms your partner might experience are some added rib pain, intense headaches, and a rising possibility of stretch marks.

Stretch marks often occur when the skin stretches quickly—both men and women can get them anytime in life, but they occur in 60-90% of pregnant women. Continuing to lather on that belly butter can help to lessen them—and hey, it might even lead to something else . . ☺

Another effect of hormone fluctuations besides the headaches can be more bouts of "pregnancy brain." Remember, this is an effort by your partner's brain to help them be an extremely attentive mother—so don't worry if they leave the keys in the fridge every once in a while.

Another common symptom this week is a boost in blood pressure. If that boost gets as high as 140/90mmHg (140 over 90), however, a doctor might diagnose hypertension and be on the lookout for *preeclampsia*—a pregnancy condition marked by high blood pressure and protein in urine that can lead to premature birth.

Beyond symptoms, however, your partner might also be getting in a bit of a give-and-take rhythm with the baby. They might start to notice when the baby becomes active or what foods they seem to react to. They might even have you feel their belly when there's a particularly consistent batch of baby kicks.

It can also make a pretty cool video!

WHAT'S HAPPENING WITH YOU - VACCINATIONS & YOU

At this point in the pregnancy, a common conversation to have with your partner is about which vaccinations your partner may elect to get—and in what order. As there are a number of vaccinations and a schedule for them that doctors often recommend, it's good to look through the list and decide which vaccines, and the timeline for receiving them. Here is a common list of vaccines recommended by doctors for your partner:

Routine (common) Vaccinations	Recommended before Pregnancy	Recommended during Pregnancy
Flu shot	Yes	Yes, if you didn't get it before pregnancy
Hepatitis A	Maybe	Maybe
Hepatitis B	Maybe	Maybe
Hib	Maybe	Maybe
HPV	Maybe, through age 26	No
MMR	Maybe	No
Meningococcal	Maybe	Maybe

Routine (common) Vaccinations	Recommended before Pregnancy	Recommended during Pregnancy
Pneumococcal	Maybe	Maybe
Td	Maybe	Maybe (better to get Tdap)
Tdap	Maybe (better to get during pregnancy	Yes, during every pregnancy (If you don't get it during pregnancy, get it right after giving birth)
Varicella	Maybe	No
Zoster	No	No

Here is a common list of vaccines recommended by doctors for your baby (keep in mind that these schedule recommendations can vary by country).

Vaccination	Birth	1 Month	2 Months	4 Months	6 Months	12 Months	15 Months	18 Months	24 Months	4 to 6 Years
HepB	1st	2nd			3rd					
DTaP			1st	2nd	3rd		4th			5th
Hib			1st	2nd	3rd	4th				
IPV			1st	2nd		3rd				4th
RV			1st	2nd	3rd					
PCV13			1st	2nd	3rd	4th				
Flu					1 or 2 doses each year					
MMR						1st				2nd
Varicella						1st				2nd
HepA						1st and 2nd				

Beyond the typical vaccine schedule, many doctors are also recommending the COVID-19 vaccination if it hasn't already been taken—but be sure to talk to your healthcare provider to see what they say before making your decision.

REFLECTIONS FROM OUR DADS

"My wife got the first dose of the COVID vaccine when she was pregnant but hadn't found out about it yet. After that, because it was so early on, there was a bit of hesitancy about getting the second dose but we ultimately decided to. At the time it was because of the limited research available, but I think what's more impactful is hearing multiple opinions from medical professionals when you just wished for a standard definitive answer. Luckily that answer seems to have become agreed upon over time and both my wife and baby are doing well!"

\- Dean F. Kansas, US.

"Never forget that almost everyone will lend you stuff. The hardest stuff was finding good stuff second hand!"

-Jon P. London, UK.

"My wife has chosen not to take the COVID vaccine due to conflicting information about it for pregnant people, and to be honest I've been feeling more anxious that as things are opening up again, and my wife isn't vaccinated, that she will have to be the only person who now has to isolate."

\- Fred S. London, UK.

☑ WEEKLY CHECKLIST

☐ Take an in-person or virtual tour of where you might have the baby!
   ☐ Get to know the vending machine locations (and snack options).

☐ Talk with your partner about vaccines for both her and the baby, and see what sort of plan or schedule you can start to make.

☐ Find out your partner's *Rh* status with her blood type—you can be either positive or negative but it's important to know if, for example, your partner is Rh negative and the baby is Rh positive.

ADIEU, SECOND TRIMESTER!

TERMS TO KNOW

Neurons – Special little cells that transmit information inside the brain.

Synapses – The point of connection between neurons where the information travels.

MOTHER AND BABY

At Week 27, your baby is now as big as a head of lettuce (14.4 inches & 1.9 pounds/.9 kg), and they are prepping for the third trimester by growing, growing, and more growing! Doctors still don't actually agree on the exact lengths of the trimesters, but a fairly common standard across the board is the third trimester beginning on Week 28. But this week, Week 27, your baby is as active as ever, trying to balance workouts and eating—but definitely mostly eating. Your partner can likely feel the increased activity, and might even cause a sudden uptick of those really niche pregnancy cravings.

Bring on the 2 a.m. fried pickle runs!!

However, more than movement and packing on the pounds, your baby is all about the brain this week. Their brain is making trillions of connections (synaptic responses) like never before. They're connecting the dots and showing tons of activity as the world is really becoming something tangible around them.

And for more good news, survivability outside the womb has jumped up to 90% as we move into the third trimester.

Your partner is likely settling into the third trimester, and preparing mentally. Just as there's a lot going on in your mind (which we're about to get into), there's likely a ton going on in your partner's. Everything that felt less real, or maybe even distant, now feels infinitely closer. However, those mental preoccupations don't account for the only changes this week.

In addition to many of the symptoms we've mentioned like Braxton Hicks, hemorrhoids, and constipation, your partner might also be experiencing even more back problems this week—ones that don't even seem to get better with lying down. That can make getting comfortable while sleeping a lot harder—and make them very thankful to have a body pillow (or maybe *you*).

Try to help them lessen the amount of time on their feet to prevent those aches and more swelling. It also might be a good time to invest in a *belly support belt* that can help carry the extra weight.

One last thing to keep an eye out for is uncontrollable peeing. Whether from sneezing, laughing, or even coughing, the baby putting so much pressure on the bladder can cause more than a little pee to sneak out. Just like back-up shirts for unexpected lactations, add some back-up pants and keep them in your car!

WHAT'S HAPPENING WITH YOU - THE LAST LEG OF THE RACE

Here it is, the end of the second trimester and moving into the last leg of this race. Your baby had the head start at the beginning, but you're caught up now. You know what to expect, you know how to handle some of the symptoms, and you're prepared for what's coming. There's still more to learn and plan for, and quite a few last-minute preparations to make sure you're ready, but all the groundwork is laid.

It's already been six months, only three more before your baby arrives!

You're doing great, so let's get ready to kick it into the homestretch.

REFLECTIONS FROM OUR DADS

"Most of Instagram is full of women going through stuff, but a man goes through it all too - as we're trying to make it right for our partners and babies. It's important that dads-to-be who are finding things stressful shout out about it more in my opinion."
- Keneal P. London, UK

"We did Antenatal classes and Hypnobirthing. It's strange because everything in those classes and processes is about this one specific day. The Mum bag, Dad bag, everything was bout getting those things ready."
- Jon P. London, UK.

"My wife and I talked a lot about the common complaints you hear from first time parents-midnight feedings, the changings, and whatnot. But, when it came down to it, we fundamentally didn't understand what those parents were talking about. There was absolutely no time that we did any of those routine things where we would have preferred an alternative, a life where we didn't have the kid. We just feel so thankful to have her. That's it."
- Lee H. South Carolina, US.

☑ WEEKLY CHECKLIST

☐ Celebrate another trimester in the books!

☐ Start thinking about post-birth pediatricians or care.

☐ Make sure you're scheduled to join a prenatal class or birthing class— whether that's in person or online. The third trimester is the perfect time.

☐ Continue discussing your birth plan as you prepare for the last trimester.

PART THREE

THE THIRD TRIMESTER

YOU'RE GOING TO BE A DAD!

Here you are, the last third of this pregnancy marathon! The third trimester, which covers Weeks 28 until birth (targeted at Week 40 but sometimes sooner or later), can feel like both the longest and shortest phase of the pregnancy. As we've already said a few times before, **your baby is calling the shots,** and **time is relative.**

Barring any pre-planned inductions or emergencies, if they decide to arrive early, that's what they decide. If they feel cozied up and want to stay a bit longer, that's their call. No matter when they're born, viability has jumped up to almost 100% this month, and that is some amazing (and infinitely relieving) news!

The third trimester is all about making plans—and making yourself flexible with those plans. You might have a birth plan, but that plan might change. You might have clear, written-down, and refined objectives, but you might need to adapt on the fly. These are the months when you take the famous birthing classes, when you put the finishing touches on the nursery, and when you start to assemble your "go-bag."

That's the third trimester: your baby has all the paint on their canvas, and now they're organizing, editing, and refining the masterpiece that is their life. They're so excited to show you all the hard work they've been doing, and we know both you and your partner are excited to meet them too. She might be feeling a resurgence of fatigue and nausea from the first trimester, but also a change in psychology with the finish line of the pregnancy now in sight.

The third trimester is here. Get ready, get prepared, and get excited—your baby is almost here!

CHAPTER SEVEN

MONTH SEVEN

Month 7 is the first month of the third trimester, and your baby's brain has kicked into high gear preparing for its first breath outside the womb. It's like a computer that just turned on and is ready to explore the hard drives for everything it can. More than just brain activity, your baby will be blinking, breathing, and—most exciting—dreaming!

What on earth is your baby dreaming about in there?

What connections does their brain make already? Is it the sounds of the music you've been playing, your voice, the smell of amniotic fluid? Or something else? It seems wild that their brain is already setting up to play and be creative before it even recognizes what there is to be creative about.

More than just expanding brain tissue, your baby will grow even more hair this month and store even more brown fat. However, because they're really packing on the pounds, your partner's body is doing everything it can to supply proper nutrients to carry the baby to term.

This month, your partner's uterus and stomach will stretch to its limit, and that can make a lot of general self-care and daily routines a real challenge. She might feel the onset of serious fatigue, insomnia, and a never-ending desire to pee as the baby is putting pressure on her bladder. Stay strong, stay proactive, and keep an open dialogue about the mixed emotions you're both feeling leading up to delivery, because here we are: **the third trimester.**

DREAM ON, BABY

TERMS TO KNOW

Prenatal Class – Classes that prepare you and your partner for what to expect with childbirth. These are known as either birthing, prenatal, or antenatal classes.

Lamaze Class – A specific brand of birthing class that helps pregnant women prepare for childbirth mentally and physically; lots of breathing exercises and hands-on practice.

Sulci & Gyri – Grooves, folds, and little indentations in the brain.

MOTHER AND BABY

The start of the third trimester and your baby is the size of an eggplant, a.k.a. an aubergine (14.8 inches & 2.2 pounds/1 kg). This week, the baby's brain is forming its very distinct ridges (called the *sulci* and *gyri*). Neurons are firing, synapses are connecting, and the baby's young mind is unveiling an entirely new world before their newly opened eyes. Because of all that amazing progress in the brain, the baby is now dreaming during sleep cycles. Early observations of fetuses in the womb have shown their eyelids fluttering, and neural readings showed activity during REM (Rapid Eye Movement) sleep. There's no way to know what your baby is dreaming about, but it's fun to imagine the possibilities...

At over two pounds, no doubt your partner is feeling the weight this week. Only a few weeks ago, the baby was the size of a coconut, and now it's likely they feel like a whole bundle of them. Cue the dreams of tropical getaways and piña coladas! This not only increases your partner's total weight, but it can put some serious stress on the lower back. The belly support belts available are more helpful now than ever.

This week can also bring all sorts of different aches and pains around her body. This is mostly due to hormone fluctuations, but surprisingly, help comes in the form of moving those muscles that are aching. Yoga, walks, a nice massage from you—all can lessen the toll those hormones are taking.

It also might be time for another popular, albeit less physical, activity of the third trimester, and getting in on it sooner can be better for understanding solutions to those intermittent pains your partner is feeling . . .

WHAT'S HAPPENING WITH YOU - HELLO, PRENATAL CLASS, PT. 1

It's likely, at this point in the pregnancy, that you've spoken with your partner about what kind of delivery you're planning for. No matter what it is—a vaginal birth, a natural birth, scheduled cesarean section, or scheduled induction—there's likely a class that will give you a rundown of what to expect.

Whatever method of birth you're planning for, it's best to take a class that holds the same values that you do. Childbirth classes are there to inform both you and your partner about what to expect. A little forewarning, though. No matter how many books you read or classes you go to, nothing really prepares you for the unique cacophony of feelings, emotions, and everything else that comes from your child's birth.

That being said, a prenatal / antenatal class is likely to cover:

- Continued steps to take to ensure a healthy pregnancy

- Mental health for you and your partner during and after pregnancy

- The value of family and social support networks

- Understanding labor and delivery (you'll even watch live birth videos, just like sixth-grade health class, hooray!)

- How to navigate hospitals, your home, or birthing centers for delivery day

- All the necessary supplies if you're planning for a homebirth

- The possibilities of medical intervention whether giving birth at a hospital, birthing center, or at home

- Some techniques for relaxation and pain-relief, like massages, breathing practices, and when and where to use warm water

- An overview of different kinds of birthing positions

- The options available for pain relief, like an epidural or natural solutions

- How best to craft your very own birth plan—and stick to it

- How to change a diaper/nappy and swaddle!

- Everything you and your partner need to know about breastfeeding

- Caring for a newborn

It's a fairly long list of possible lessons, and it's highly recommended that you attend at least one of these classes (though most can occur one day a week for a month or more). Yes, they can be boring at times. Yes, the videos they show are pretty explicit, but at least now you might have a much better understanding of what to expect. But one thing a prenatal class offers that can outshine nearly everything else—**friends!**

A prenatal class is often one of the first times new and expecting parents can meet other new and expecting parents. You can finally talk to adults about everything you've been going through, and even build some long-time relationships through your experience!

So, if not for the knowledge, go for the friendships. Actually, yeah, definitely go for the knowledge too—there's so much good stuff to learn!

All that said, you still have a bit of time, but it's very common to sign up for the class in the seventh month.

REFLECTIONS FROM OUR DADS

"We planned to have a home birth but ended up getting induced in the hospital! My wife had a complication called colistasis, where her liver got overwhelmed with all the estrogen and started to shut down—very bad for her and baby! The Pitocin kicked in so fast that she basically went from zero to sixty, and after eight hours of heavy labor, she opted for the epidural—which was definitely NOT in our plan! But in the end, we were so grateful to have a hospital birth. Our son spent the first six days in the NICU with a lung infection, so it was amazing to be right there to get him the care he needed."
- Keith G. Seattle, US.

"When I started to see the bump and the baby started kicking. That's when Amy and I started to get even closer."
- William F. Leicester, UK

☑ WEEKLY CHECKLIST

☐ Be mindful of the third trimester's more frequent prenatal visits and plan ahead.

☐ Look into infant CPR classes. We hope you'll never have to use what you learn, but it's great to have the comfort of that knowledge.

☐ Watch your partner's belly to see if you can notice yet when your baby kicks.

☐ Talk with your partner about circumcision (if applicable) and see if it's the right choice for both of you, and your baby.

BUILDING STRONG BONES

TERMS TO KNOW

Prolactin – Hormone released in women that starts milk production after the baby is born.

Colostrum – The pre-birth leaking of 'milk'; basically pre-milk that has tons of valuable nutrients, minerals, and antibodies.

Sciatic Nerve – Major nerve that extends from the lower spine to the upper thigh and can really start to tighten and bother pregnant women.

MOTHER AND BABY

It's Week 29, and your baby is the size of a cauliflower (15.2 inches and 2.5 pounds/1.1 kg)! This week, the baby will likely be very active, and your partner will be feeling those quick one-two jab combos on her uterus. After all, your baby is training for the big day so put on the *Rocky* soundtrack to help out! As a note, that soundtrack is also fantastic for household chores. However, with your partner's uterus continuing to expand more and more, and the constant pressure from your little prizefighter on her bladder, the bathroom breaks are *even* more frequent.

The other big thing happening this week has to do with the baby's growing bones. You've probably discovered by now that the baby and your partner's relationship is give-and-take—your partner is using everything to *give* to both the baby and her own body, and the baby is *taking* whatever they can get. However, if your partner isn't able to supply the baby with enough from diet or supplements, the baby will start to take whatever they need from your partner's reserves.

For example, this week calcium is extremely important for the baby's growing bones. But if your partner doesn't have enough calcium in their diet, *how will the baby get it?* Well, they'll take it—right from their mother's bone marrow. I know, it sounds a bit harsh—but in the third trimester, the baby is doubling and tripling in weight before birth. With that rapid growth, big strong bones are just part of the equation. This is why doctors put such a big focus on calcium—if your partner doesn't have enough to offer the baby, they'll be exhausted, fatigued, and aching when the baby uses theirs.

On the plus side, an easy snack for calcium is often yogurt or fortified cereals. But beyond calcium, your partner might also be experiencing some breast leakage this week. It doesn't happen with every woman, but if it does, it comes from the production of the baby's first food, a yellowish substance called *colostrum*.

Colostrum is a bit of a test run for making milk as your partner's body prepares to release the hormone *prolactin*, but it's also extremely vital in its own right. If your partner is breastfeeding, colostrum is the first food supply for your baby, and it is packed with essential vitamins and fortifying nutrients. More than that, it is also the baby's first line of defense as it provides them with immune protection against different pathogens. Any antibody your partner has can be given to the baby through colostrum to protect them and boost their physiological growth and development. Researchers have even found if the mother has COVID-19 antibodies, they can be passed on to the baby through colostrum.

However, right now it's perfectly natural for your partner to be leaking colostrum, and keeping a spare shirt in the car or close by can help with any leaks in public.

WHAT'S HAPPENING WITH YOU - READING YOUR PARTNER

There's no way to guess how the last trimester of the pregnancy is impacting your partner. For a lot of women, the second trimester is the 'easiest' part of the pregnancy. For others, the heavy symptoms of nausea and aches just haven't seemed to let up.

At this point, you might feel you have a "good temperature of the room" when it comes to how your partner is handling the pregnancy.

And now, in the third trimester, you'll need everything you've learned so far. As much as your partner might want to go about their daily routines of seeing friends, working, running errands, exercising, or even cooking, it's completely possible that they'll feel too drained to do anything. In that way, everything you've observed so far is going to help you anticipate what your partner might be feeling next. Your partner might want more help from you, or they might want more time to themselves.

Yes, this all might get you into a zombie-like routine on occasion. You might find yourself seeing them under the covers with their pregnancy pillow and realize they haven't gotten their nightly cup of water, their heating pad, or their prenatal vitamin. In that way, many dads-to-be can feel some extreme caretaking instincts develop in this stage of pregnancy.

The truth is, many of us have never experienced that kind of caretaking before. As much as it's a great precursor to taking care of a baby (who requires as much attention as you can possibly offer), this stage can wear on a lot of first-time dads. If you feel stressed or overworked, don't be afraid to talk to someone. If not your partner, seek out a friend or family member. Sometimes just venting your feelings can offer some respite.

Don't forget to do your best to make time for the things that keep you feeling good too. If that's more sleep, try to see how you can manage your time to get more. If that's exercise, see where it can fit into your schedule. If that's simply unwinding on the couch, don't feel bad about needing those moments to yourself.

REFLECTIONS FROM OUR DADS

"Not everything is a battle. That really helped me during the pregnancy, and even after. I don't have to stress about every little thing because even if it were a battle I couldn't win every time. I wanted to be this super version of myself, Superdad; but with work commitments, I couldn't make every appointment. And that was okay. I let myself off the hook, and was sure to be present where I could. It was clinging to a false sense of control that was ultimately not feasible."

- Mason C. Maine, US.

☑ WEEKLY CHECKLIST

- ☐ Take some time to yourself to reflect on
  becoming a first-time dad:
  - ☐ Maybe go on a hike, a drive, or just take
    a day to relax.
  - ☐ Enjoy some of your favorite foods.
  - ☐ Focus on all the positives that this new chapter will bring
    but be honest about the changes you can anticipate.

WEEK

30

SECONDS, PLEASE!

TERMS TO KNOW

Fetal Non-Stress Test (NST) – This test will check your baby's heart rate while they respond to movements.

Fetal Kick Count Test – Test to check for baby movement over a short period of time (typically two hours).

Cord Blood Banking – Storing blood from the umbilical cord, rich in a lot of helpful stem cells, before the birth; in other words, while it's still attached inside and baby is still using it.

MOTHER AND BABY

Week 30, can you believe it? Your baby is the length of a zucchini/ courgette (15.7 inches & 2.9 pounds/1.3 kg), and it's getting a little crowded in there! They are eating non-stop, absorbing all the vital nutrients they can and *then some*. This week, all of the baby's major organs have fully developed, and their eyes are doing even better to observe the world around them.

They can separate light and dark, even if it looks a bit like when somebody shines a flashlight at your closed eyes. Keep in mind, though, newborns can barely see more than a few inches in front of them at birth. Regardless of sight, they are still moving, kicking, jabbing, and hiccuping—and your partner is probably getting used to the non-stop rave inside her uterus.

On that note, this week marks a bit of a change. Where before it was strange to feel the baby moving, now it's strange to *not* feel movement. It's important to keep in mind that the baby's sleep cycle is determined mostly by comfort (such as being lulled to sleep from walking), but non-movement for too long can sometimes feel alarming to mothers—so much so that they'll coax a little movement from the baby. To which baby responds: "Hey now, I'm in here! Quit poking!"

That said, if your partner does notice a lack of movement for an extended period of time, many doctors will recommend a small test for fetal movement before coming in for a check. This is sometimes called a *Fetal Kick Count Test*. To do it, they'll recommend drinking a juice (often orange juice but something with a little sugar) and then having your partner lie on her left side. Over the course of two hours, with very little other movement, your partner tries to gauge if they feel at least ten kicks from the baby. If they do, there's no cause for alarm. If they don't, it's best to go see your doctor for more testing or a wellness check.

Luckily, this week the baby is also able to activate some of those strong neck muscles and turn their head from rays of sunlight or that light poke on the belly. Your partner, on the other hand, might be experiencing aches quite literally *all over*. The hips, joints, back, feet, and belly can all start to give off a general throbbing of achy-breaky pain this week. That can be compounded if your partner is having trouble sleeping, which gives their body some time to repair and restore itself.

To get ahead of the aches, do whatever you can to keep her comfortable, even if it means mustering the energy to give a massage after your own hard day. If possible, more time with the heating pad, more use from the support belt, and more cuddling with the pregnancy pillow can all help. The comfort trifecta!

WHAT'S HAPPENING WITH YOU - HELLO, PRENATAL CLASS, PT. 2

It feels like we were just talking about birthing classes, but here we are with another bit of information on the subject. This time, it's important to talk about how prenatal classes have evolved since COVID-19.

As mentioned previously, COVID has become another condition to think about when it comes to pregnancy, but it shouldn't necessarily be any more worrisome than others. When the pandemic was at its peak, people didn't suddenly stop having babies. We all had to adapt. Mothers were required to wear masks in the delivery room, visitation was limited (even for the fathers), and prenatal classes moved online.

Although the peak of the pandemic is hopefully behind us, some changes have lingered. Many prenatal classes are still entirely online, and some have altered their syllabus to include birthing, delivery, and childcare in a post-COVID world. Depending on where you are, and the local policies around COVID, you're likely to experience a few changes when it comes to hospital stays and guest visitations, as many hospitals and birthing centers have grown warier of potential outbreaks in the future.

Many of these subjects will be covered in prenatal classes, but again, these classes also might have less of a hands-on approach if they are taken online. For some, that's a nice relief (information download from a distance). For others, less hands-on means more questions upon delivery. However, many are offering hybrid workshops that combine in-person and online elements.

It may take a bit more research to find the right prenatal class for you, but the right one is definitely out there!

REFLECTIONS FROM OUR DADS

"It was all so unpredictable, especially with managing pregnancy through any restrictions. You don't know how to deal with things. You've got a whole load of things you're thinking about. How will I be able to manage everything. Plus you don't know what to really expect."
- Simon H. Stratford-Upon-Avon, UK.

"I had a lot of people telling me to watch out for the mood swings, but I don't know, my wife seemed to keep a fairly level head throughout the whole process. That's always been a staple of her personality though."
- James E.Florida, US.

☑ WEEKLY CHECKLIST

☐ Make sure you have a plan in place for labor
and delivery:

    ☐ If it applies, practice driving to the
hospital to see how long it takes and the
fastest route and reach out to a friend or family member
to watch the house (or pet-sit) while you're away.

☐ Talk with your partner and research the possibility of cord blood
banking to see if it's something you're interested in doing.

WEEK

31

LIGHTNING IN A BOTTLE

TERMS TO KNOW

Lightning Crotch – Sharp, shooting, almost completely unexplainable pain in the pelvic region of pregnant women; not a fun time at all.

Oligohydramnios – Condition with too little amniotic fluid around the baby; only occurs in 4% of pregnancies.

Polyhydramnios – Condition with too much amniotic fluid around the baby; only occurs in 1-2% of pregnancies.

MOTHER AND BABY

At thirty-one weeks, your baby is the size of an asparagus bundle (16.2 inches and 3.3 pounds/1.5 kg)! This is also an exciting week because it officially marks the last week of (very) pre-term pregnancy. If the baby is delivered any time after this week, viability has skyrocketed to 99% as they enter the moderate pre-term range.

We really are in the homestretch now!

This week, the baby is still doing everything it can to pack on the pounds and get those neurons firing. Their brain is in rapid development, along with skin that's quickly filling out. All the wrinkles on the baby are now fading away as the skin plumps up from the fat accumulating beneath it. And because of that fat, the  lanugo that once protected the baby by regulating their temperature is also starting to fall away and join the amniotic fluid mixture. The reason for this is that the baby's brain has now developed enough to use the fat to help them control temperature without the lanugo's help.

In addition, the baby's lungs are starting to practice more "breathing," and the eyes are starting to blink more regularly. Right now, the baby blinks about 6-to-15 times per hour (compared to adults who blink 19-20 times per minute.) We're not sure why baby blinking so slowly makes them seem even cuter (maybe like a wise-old tortoise), but it does!

Although the baby is running out of places to somersault effectively, your partner is likely still feeling those gymnast tumbles and perfect-ten dismounts. However, they might also be feeling something new this week—in addition to Braxton Hicks contractions (which can now sometimes easily be confused with real ones) is the ever-so-kindly dubbed "lightning crotch."

That's right, lightning crotch is a thing, and it's horrible. Doctors can't even explain it yet. It's just like it sounds. Basically, lightning crotch is a sudden, drop-to-your-knees, cry out from sharp, shooting pain in the pelvic region that happens to some pregnant women. Bottom line, it definitely ain't fun. If it shows up, there isn't much you can do to help other than have her ride the wave and maybe have a nice treat together afterward.

Beyond that, if your partner is still having some trouble sleeping, it might be a good time to address how comfortable the bedroom is for them. It could be something as simple as diffusing some essential oils (lavender, if your doctor approves) or taking the hit of lowering the thermostat a couple of degrees cooler.

WHAT'S HAPPENING WITH YOU - SAVORING TIME

We're coming to the end of the first month of the third trimester, and the baby is set to arrive in only a few weeks' time. It may happen slowly, but by now it's likely sinking in that your world is about to be forever changed. We don't say that to scare you, only to let you know that the next chapter of your life is about to start.

It's going to be a rewarding, challenging, and beautiful part of your life. But it can also mean saying goodbye to a lot of your old life— this part you're living right now, before the baby and before you're officially a dad. Maybe you've been wanting and praying and wishing to be a father for years, and it's finally happening. Or maybe you're not sure you're ready just yet. Hey, it might even be both.

Your baby coming into the world isn't going to stop you from doing the things you love, but it will very likely cause you to adapt. If you haven't already, make a list or a plan of something you want to do. It could be a babymoon with your partner if you haven't already taken one. It could be a nice night out with friends. It could be relaxing for a full day and watching movies, sports, playing video games, writing, drawing, or practicing music. The point of savoring this time isn't to say goodbye to any of this stuff. All of it will still be there, even when you have a baby in the world.

The only difference is, even if you don't notice it right now, the priorities you have in life might irrevocably shift, if only just a little bit. We can't say for sure how having a baby will affect you, but we know that it *will*. So take stock this week and express what you're thankful for—and what you're hopeful for.

REFLECTIONS FROM OUR DADS

"I couldn't voice my stress during the pregnancy. I couldn't say to anyone I'm tired and fearful. I didn't have a support network aside from my wife – who was going through a lot too. I felt frustrated, especially when all people are asking is 'how's mum?' It's alright to say that 'I'm struggling with this' - and more dads-to-be should speak up if they feel that way too."

- Kristopher F, Greenock Inverclyde, Scotland.

"Every single day we did the same walk around. I think we went out twice a day - the walk around became a good daily habit. We used that time to really talk about the baby. It's been something we've carried on post birth."

- Simon H. Stratford-Upon-Avon, UK

☑ WEEKLY CHECKLIST

☐ If you have pets, start thinking about preparing them for the baby! Pets aren't always welcoming to a new member in the house, so to get them prepared, it's good to keep a few things in mind:

    ☐ Sign them up for training classes to stop any bad habits like jumping up in a crib or tearing up clothes or toys.

    ☐ Take them to vet for any possible vaccine updates.

    ☐ Have other babies visit if you can to get them used to the sound of crying or a lack of attention being given to them.

    ☐ After the birth, bring home a sock or hat or something that smells like them to get them used to the scent of your baby ahead of time.

☐ Be aware of some of the signs of **preterm labor:**

    ☐ Lower back pain or discomfort.

    ☐ Intense pelvic pressure.

    ☐ Abdominal cramping or regular contractions (if she is having four to six contractions an hour, it's time to call the doctor!).

    ☐ Vaginal spotting or bleeding.

    ☐ Vaginal discharge (anything resembling the mucus plug).

    ☐ Fluid leakage (it could be a sign that her water broke early).

CHAPTER EIGHT

MONTH EIGHT

The countdown is real! Only two months to go! Your baby is continuing to pack on the fat in preparation for delivery, and that ultimately means a good bit of extra weight your partner is carrying around too. Just imagine bringing up that box full of old pictures and memories from the basement, resting them on your belt to support the weight, and then *never being* able to set it down, for *months*.

In other words, carrying a baby can feel like a workout every hour of every day.

By now, your partner has likely become accommodated to the hardships of fashion and the plethora of symptoms. A lot of women can experience an intense mixture of nerves, stress, and eager anticipation this month. The best thing you can do is work together to balance any of those stressors. That might take the form of meditation, breathing exercises, slow walks, listening to music, or just unwinding on the couch in free moments you can spare.

There are no right or wrong answers, but when you're not chasing moments of solitude, do your best to have conversations with your partner about the decisions that are fast approaching. *What's the birth plan? Cloth or disposable diapers? Circumcision or not?* All these choices are coming up. We'll cover some in more detail, but it's best to start thinking about them now.

You're doing great so far, let's keep on trucking!

contractions might even become more common this week. *Practice makes perfect, right? Maybe?* She might also experience a good bit of heartburn as well as some added fatigue—or maybe the excitement of baby coming soon is dimming those symptoms.

In the case of high-risk pregnancy, Week 32 is also when your doctor will likely do a complete biophysical profile. Just like it sounds, it's an intense check-up (specifically an ultrasound) that measures amniotic fluid to make sure everything is within acceptable parameters. Week 32 is also often when you're getting used to more frequent doctor visits and check-ups, making sure everything is going at the pace it should.

You might even learn for sure if the baby has turned head-down!

WHAT'S HAPPENING WITH YOU - BABY SHOWERS & BABY ESSENTIALS

There are no hard and fast rules for if or when to have a baby shower, but they are most common between four and eight weeks before delivery. That way, your partner is far enough along for safety, but they aren't so far along that there could be an untimely delivery at the party. However, you're still likely not invited to the baby shower.

Yes, there are some baby showers that feature dads, but a majority of them are made, and hosted, by mothers and for mothers. It can feel a bit strange to be excluded from a celebration for the baby you made together, and it will likely change in the coming years—but for now, if you want to be involved with the baby shower, you might need to make it known. Otherwise, it's just not terribly likely that you'll get the invite.

On the plus side, some dads throw "Diaper Parties." It's basically an excuse to hang out with a good group of your best mates, but they buy you a few diapers alongside the drinks and snacks they bring. Whatever you call it, don't miss out on a fun night!

This is also a good time to mention the essentials that you're going to need in the coming weeks. We have three to mention, and we think they're vital:

The Go Bag and/or Diaper/Nappy Bag

We mentioned it before but we can't express how important this bag is for you. It's going to hold all of the baby's odds and ends, as well as your own. The first chance you get to use it is when the baby is born!

If you need a full list of what to fill your go-bag with, check out Week 38!

The Carrier

More than just carrying your baby's things, you need something to carry your baby too—and that's where a carrier comes in. There are different styles from swaddles and full-on harnesses, but there's no better way to conveniently hold your baby while also having them cuddle close to you. If we could recommend anything, get one with good leg support for your baby.

Diapers vs. Reusables

Here's the debate. You're either going to need a ton of diapers/nappies, or a few reusables and a strong stomach. A lot of first-time dads love to toss out diapers rather than clean, and if that's the case, get a Diaper Genie. Just do it—you'll thank us later. However, there are no wrong answers—besides, you know, not having any diapers at all. And no one needs to experience that mistake!

REFLECTIONS FROM OUR DADS

"Our 7th month was the best. By that time Charlene was over the sickness and the bump was clearly there. We were also doing hypnobirthing. We did it religiously for 6 months everyday before the birth. The tricky thing was that the rules for hospitals were changing all the time. The hospital would allow a birth partner in, but you had to be a certain stage of labor before you were allowed in."

– Simon H. Stratford-Upon-Avon, UK.

"My partner got really uncomfortable at the end – all I could do was be available to talk. What can I make better so I batched cooked 45 meals and put them in the freezer and got a cleaner to help make the home spotless for that first day back."

– Jon P. London, UK.

" To an extent, the first 7 months felt easy – like planning a holiday. But the last couple of months – you know that from that point of view if the baby comes it's going to be fine, but it felt like 'wow – this is actually real, and what if I'm a terrible dad? What if I don't know how to hold the baby? The mind really started to go into overdrive for me."

– Robin L, London, UK.

☑ WEEKLY CHECKLIST

☐ Think about ordering a baby keepsake book for you and your partner—you can even start it up early with the ultrasound images!

☐ Install the baby's car seat!

   ☐ Take as long as you need and do it multiple times to make sure you've definitely got it safe and secure.

ANTIBODIES, IMMUNITY, & THE SKULL

TERMS TO KNOW

Fontanelle – Soft parts of the newborn skull so it can squeeze through the birth canal.

Placenta Previa – When the placenta covers the cervix (the exit), it can cause a lot of bleeding during delivery.

Antibodies – A blood protein used by the immune system to fight off bacteria and viruses.

Costochondritis – The swelling of cartilage on the inner chest wall that can cause rib pain.

MOTHER AND BABY

It's Week 33, and your baby is the size of a pineapple (17.2 inches & 4.2 pounds/1.9 kg)! Every day, the baby is growing, moving, and preparing to finally meet you. This week the biggest thing to note is on a more molecular level. As the baby readies to join the world, they're building up their immune system for protection from infections post-birth.

To do that, you guessed it, they're getting those antibodies from your partner, who is serving them up on a platter through the placenta. This is extremely important, as the baby's immune system isn't the strongest at birth. It will build up over the first few months of their lives, but in the meantime, best not to let the dog lick their face for a while (even if they so desperately want to).

Meanwhile, the baby's bones are getting stronger, harder, yet still malleable. Specifically, the baby's skull will keep its soft spot, the fontanelle, so that they can squeeze their way through a narrow birth canal. This might also be an important time to mention that your baby at birth might not look like you're expecting. More on that later, but just know they come out looking a little more like Dan Ackroyd's *Conehead* than the Hallmark babies.

Your partner might be feeling any number of symptoms this week, including increased rib pain. As the ribs are stretched out to make room for the baby, she might be feeling some sharp or dull pain. This swelling of the cartilage in the inner chest wall is called *costochondritis*. Again, the baby making more room means pressing on your partner to make that room. Late in the third trimester, that pressing and stretching of the uterus might impact the diaphragm or lungs too, and cause some further discomfort and shortness of breath.

Another common symptom this week is overheating. Right now, your partner's metabolic rate is through the roof, and that means sweating (and more shortness of breath) from almost any strenuous or exertive activity. The most important thing is to have your partner take it as easy as possible these weeks. That might mean you taking on even more of the household duties and planning—but be sure to take time for yourself too. We know, sometimes easier said than done when it feels like there's just so much to do. Step-by-step, though.

You've got this!

WHAT'S HAPPENING WITH YOU – NAIL DOWN THE BIRTH PLAN

With the delivery date fast approaching, it's more important than ever to make an official *birth plan*. A birth plan is less an actual *plan of action* for the birth and more so a list of preferences that you and your partner discuss and agree before the delivery.

The reason you make a birth plan is to open up an honest dialogue between you, your partner, and your doctor around the various options for childbirth. It also provides you with a convenient list of answers for the doctors, doulas, midwives, or anyone else that might be taking care of you. That way, when you arrive at the hospital, birthing center, or your living room, the people there understand what kind of labor and delivery you hope to experience.

Of course, most of these birth plans are designed under normal circumstances, and a lot can happen at the hospital, birthing center, or home that needs to be acted on quickly—but a birth plan helps you plan ahead for those options and know how you wish to respond to possible interventions. To help out, we've crafted our own fill-in-the-blank template to answer a few of the vital questions:

289

MY BIRTH PLAN

Basic Info

Name : _____

Partner : _____

Visitor 1 : _____

Visitor 2 : _____

Visitor 3 : _____

Visitor 4 : _____

Visitor 5 : _____

Labor & Delivery

Atmosphere :

_____

_____

_____

Pain Management :

_____

_____

_____

Preferred Birthing Position :

_____

_____

_____

In Case of Emergency :

_____

_____

_____

Doctor : _____

Midwife : _____

Social Security No : _____

Birth Date : _____

Due Date : _____

Planned Type of Delivery : _____

PMH/ Diagnosis : _____

Postpartum

Umbilical Cord :

_____

_____

_____

Baby Cleaning :

_____

_____

_____

Baby Feeding Plan :

_____

_____

_____

In Case of Emergency :

_____

_____

_____

Other Notes :

_____

_____

_____

REFLECTIONS FROM OUR DADS

"I never met our Midwife and I wasn't allowed to go to any of the appointments due to COVID-19. It wasn't necessarily great in terms of the birth plan, but we were prepared and the experience at the hospital was amazing. I ended up staying there for quite a bit after the birth."

- Matteo V. Surrey, UK.

"A week before the birth – Sarah was feeling pretty low because she developed a condition called obstetric cholestasis (OC) which caused her to suffer from rabid itching."

- Adam I. London, UK.

☑ WEEKLY CHECKLIST

☐ Make sure you and your partner are signed up or have already taken your prenatal, birthing, and possibly CPR class.

☐ Start to pack your go-bag!
  ☐ Check out Week 38 for the complete list.

☐ Inquire about some of the hospital resources for new moms, such as lactation consultants.

☐ Finalize the birth plan!

ADD VERNIX TO THE BOWL-YUM!

TERMS TO KNOW

Breech (a.k.a carrying breech) – When a baby is born feet-first rather than head-first.

Caesarean Section (C-Section) – Surgical procedure to deliver the baby by cutting into the mother's abdomen and uterus.

MOTHER AND BABY

Week 34 means your baby is about the size of a cantaloupe (17.7 inches & 4.4 pounds/2 kg)! This week, the lungs are on their final stretch of development, and the amniotic fluid typically hits its all-time high (about one-and-a-half pints!). The baby is swimming in it, swallowing it, and even (in a manner of speaking) "breathing" it in. They're using all its vital nutrients to put the finishing touches on any remaining development—think of it like the final glaze and maybe a few sprinkles on the doughnut.

Because of this huge influx of amniotic fluid, it's also taking up a lot of space in your partner's belly. By now, her uterus has expanded up to 1,000 times its initial size. That's insane! Your partner no doubt has felt that stretching in increments all these long months, but this week those ligaments surrounding the uterus are now relaxing a bit to prepare for delivery.

Your baby is almost here!

However, even now, the baby and your partner are still finding their rhythm together. The baby's sleep patterns might be in sync or completely opposite to your partner, the bladder pile-drivers might still feel completely random (and show up at the worst possible times), and the uptick in activity might be a welcome surprise after certain meals. This week, your partner might be feeling constipation and abdominal pressure causing even more frequent urination. At least *something* is coming out. If the constipation gets bad enough, adding further pressure on her belly, focus on those fiber-rich snacks and foods—and nothing helps move things around like a steady walk.

This week also might feature another nice HD ultrasound of the baby where you can really see the definition of their face and all those fingers and toes wiggling around. The more you see the baby, the more it all feels real.

WHAT'S HAPPENING WITH YOU - BEING THEIR VOICE & ADVOCATE

There's a big role you're about to take on for your partner when you get to the delivery room (wherever that happens to be). Your role is to *be their advocate.*

During labor and delivery, there is going to be a whirlwind of information coming to both you and your partner all at once. There will be things to remember, and there will be people to talk to. Before you get to that stage, have an honest and open conversation with your partner about their expectations with delivery. It is very likely that she might be in too much pain or otherwise unable to answer the doctors' questions.

Because of that, *you need to know those answers and express them.*

Your partner might have said to you, "Under no circumstances do I want an epidural. Even if I'm begging, pleading, and crying—do not let them give me one."

What do you do in that situation?

What do you do when you see them in pain? Did you talk to them more about how you might be feeling to see them in any severe amount of pain, and how that feeling might impact your decision in the moment?

That's the key.

During labor and after delivery, your partner is likely to be extremely exhausted. You need to be their voice and their advocate. Will you check in with the doctors? Will you ensure your partner gets skin-to-skin contact she asked for immediately after birth? Will you keep up with what's happening with the baby during any measurements or outside the room observations? Will you look over any paperwork that needs to be read or signed? After the birth, when parents or loved ones come to visit, will you tell them if your partner is too tired for visitors? These different instances of labor and afterward need to be talked about with your partner.

You also have some big things to consider for yourself:

Do you want to be there to watch the baby being born?

Do you want to be holding your partner's hand or standing by their side?

Do you want to be the one to cut the umbilical cord?

Do you want to catch the baby?

All these questions and situations can arise during delivery and after—the more you can answer and prepare for, the less stress the entire endeavor will bring both you and your partner.

REFLECTIONS FROM OUR DADS

"It was four in the morning and my wife was exhausted. She asked for the epidural, and I very gently reminded her that it wasn't part of our plan. In no uncertain terms she told me the plan was out the window! In the end, the epidural was exactly what she needed."
- Keith G. Seattle, US.

"When you feel the kicks – It's a weird moment when he was doing somersaults in her tummy. Towards the back end of the pregnancy I was putting my hand on it and feeling that full force of the kick too which was incredible."
- Rob S. York, UK..

☑ WEEKLY CHECKLIST

☐ Talk over your birth plan with your doctor or midwife and make sure they have a copy to keep themselves.

    ☐ Be conscious of questions about:

        ☐ Episiotomies.

        ☐ Epidurals.

        ☐ C-Sections.

        ☐ High-Risk Concerns or Possible Interventions.

        ☐ Skin-to-Skin Contact.

        ☐ Cutting the Cord or Delayed Clamping.

        ☐ Placenta Delivery.

        ☐ COVID Guest restrictions.

☐ If it applies, help write those baby shower 'thank you' notes.

☐ Talk to your partner to make sure you know everything you need to know about what they want or hope for during the birth.

☐ This is a great week to make sure all your earlier preparations for your home are in order or this week they're receiving their finishing touches.

    ☐ Ready to Go Checklist:

        ☐ Nursery completed.

        ☐ Birth Plan Prepared.

☐ Tested the "systems" like a diaper/nappy station to make sure they're ready and you know how to use them.

 ☐ Go-bag prepared (Week 38 has the full list of essentials).

 ☐ Newborn car seat installed.

 ☐ Route to hospital, birthing center, or home set-up plotted and planned.

WEEK

35

APPROACHING THE
HOMESTRETCH

TERMS TO KNOW

Epidural – An injection (with a large needle) into the spine to block labor pains and contractions.

External Cephalic Version (ECV) – Procedure to turn a breech (feet-first) baby head-down.

Episiotomy (perineotomy) - A small incision made below the vagina to reduce the possibility of tearing during pregnancy.

MOTHER AND BABY

Week 35—the last week before the
last month and your baby is the size
of a honeydew melon (18.2 inches
& 5.3 pounds/2.4 kg)! This week  is
a great milestone for the baby's
development as they officially move
from moderate pre-term to late pre-term. At this point, they have
99% viability, and babies have a great chance of breathing on their
own without assistance from here on out. This is because they've
had a lot of amniotic fluid to work with, which reached its peak last
week, and their little lungs are finally strong enough to take that first
breath.

In addition to the lungs, other vital organs are starting to take over
their responsibilities. The kidneys are now producing sterile urine
(and a lot of it) which, just like previously, still re-enters the amniotic
fluid and offers the baby continued nutrients.

However, they're not the only one dealing with excess urine. Very
often at this stage, your partner may not only experience frequent
urination (tell them something they don't know), but they also
might experience *leaking urine* that's often brought on by stress
and constant bladder pressure. During the weeks before delivery,
your partner may be feeling a whirlwind of emotions: attachment to
pregnancy, desire for it to be done, worries about delivery, and/or
just an overall exhaustion.

As mentioned, the baby is resting a little lower now on your partner's
uterus as they prepare for birth, and that might put some added
pressure on her lower back too. This is the time where movement for

your partner should be relatively minimal and any proactive help you can offer is greatly appreciated.

It also might be a good time to talk with healthcare providers and your partner about a perineal massage—a specific type of massage designed to stretch the perineal tissue (between vagina and rectum) to prevent possible tearing during delivery. If that is something your partner is interested in, it is becoming increasingly more common and can also help prevent the need for an *episiotomy* (also commonly referred to as a *perineotomy*), which is a small incision made below the vagina to reduce the possibility of tearing during pregnancy. We'll cover more on this in a later chapter, but for now, having all the conversations as early as possible is more helpful in the long run.

The last month of pregnancy has arrived, and to make sure you're ready here is...

WHAT'S HAPPENING WITH YOU - THE FOUR STAGES OF LABOR

Even though we're not officially in Month 9 yet, it's definitely time to go over the stages of labor in case they sneak up on you at 3 a.m. while you're snuggled up under the covers. Even if you wake up in a total daze, knowing the signs ahead of time will help your own instincts kick in, as well as your partner's!

Just a quick heads up, the stages of labor, like most anything else in pregnancy, will be different for each individual. There is no real predictive measure for how long any given stage will last, but certain things like a *planned induction* might be used to make the stages more predictable or controlled. Additionally, if your partner has a *planned C-section*—many of these stages might not necessarily apply, unless the C-section is being used as an emergency surgery measure rather than a scheduled surgery.

With that in mind...

The First Stage

The first stage of labor is marked by the thinning (effacement) and opening (dilation) of your partner's cervix. The way you know it's happening is by contractions. The hard thing to differentiate is whether these are the "real deal" contractions or the false-start Braxton Hicks contractions.

The first stage of labor itself is also split into three parts.

Early Labor – "Is this Labor?!"

In early labor, the cervix opens up to about four centimeters. For the most part, you're still at home for this part of labor. The contractions are often spread out, relatively light, and could be twenty or more minutes apart. It's the stage of labor where you're still not positive and your partner might be asking, "Is this it?"

Eventually, though, these contractions will get closer together (five minutes apart or less), and that's when your partner moves into...

Active Labor – "This is DEFINITELY Labor!"

Active labor is where the cervix opens to about seven centimeters, and it is now time to get to your birthing location. Contractions are often between four and five minutes apart and can last up to a minute! It's going to get harder for your partner to walk and talk at this stage, and her water might break at any moment. Play music in the car, listen to what she needs, and get where you need to go.

Whenever you arrive to the hospital, this is also likely the stage of labor where they will offer things like Pitocin (synthetic oxytocin) to encourage labor, and/or an *epidural* (a local anesthetic) meant to lessen the pain of labor—but the decision is left to your partner (or you as their advocate) and the doctor when and if to receive these options.

Transition to the Second Stage – Getting Prepared to Push!

The transition stage is often one of the shortest stages of labor, but it's also one of the most painful. Many women experience vomiting or extreme shaking. This is the stage where you're there to offer as much support as you possibly can. You helped get them to the place they need to be for delivery, now it's about holding their hand, massaging them if they ask, listening to their needs, bringing water, or maybe holding a cold rag to their forehead.

This stage is tough, and the end of it means your partner is fully dilated, which also means . . .

The Second Stage

This is the stage where women will often find themselves experiencing an uncontrollable urge to push. With no previous interventions like an epidural that numbs the lower body, a woman will often feel an "overwhelming need to push" naturally to birth the baby. This stage can be quick or last for hours, and the baby's arrival marks the end of it. Which brings us to . . .

The Third Stage

In the third stage of labor, your baby has arrived into the world, but there's still one thing left to come out—the placenta. That's right, the baby's life-giving companion has to be birthed as well. A placenta will often be pushed out naturally, but it could take anywhere from a few minutes to a few hours.

The Fourth Stage

And finally, the fourth stage of labor is the recovery period. The postpartum stage is where your partner's body heals and slowly changes back to nearly how it was before the pregnancy. But let's not get too far ahead of ourselves just yet...

REFLECTIONS FROM OUR DADS

"I had my first child before COVID and I was present for everything. But with my second child, my son, I couldn't be there and I was sad to not be as involved. My wife even bought a portable heart beat monitor as a gift for my birthday just so I could finally listen to our baby at 7 months pregnancy. It really helped with the experience and thankfully they allowed me in for labor— albeit in a full body suit."

- Jan T. Warsaw, Poland

"We had an emergency C-section at 35 weeks. I was there for the delivery but then immediately kicked out. The medical team became quite panicked during the birth, and it was horrendous. I wouldn't wish that on my worst enemy."

- Ben B. Norwich, UK.

"At 35 weeks we had our first real scare. Amy (my partner) suffers from diabetes, and after they did some tests they decided to keep her in hospital. All the signs were that they were delivering her now! She was on a drip for 12 hours. And neither of us were getting any answers. That was the biggest frustration."

- William F. Leicester, UK.

☑ WEEKLY CHECKLIST

- ☐ Ask about the *Group-B Strep Test* and when to schedule it.
- ☐ Be aware of some of the signs of labor:
  - ☐ Contractions that increase and decrease with baby activity, are centered around the pelvic area, and arrive at regular intervals. Use the app to keep track—if they occur every five minutes or closer and each lasts more than 45 seconds, labor is starting!
  - ☐ Severe cramping.
  - ☐ Lower back pain.
  - ☐ Mucus plug dropping out and the "bloody show."
  - ☐ Blood-tinged vaginal discharge.
  - ☐ And rupturing of the amniotic sac "water breaking" is a sign of **active labor!**

CHAPTER NINE

MONTH NINE

Here it is. Hopefully the last month of pregnancy. It feels surreal to be here, but your baby is anxiously waiting to meet you, and no doubt you and your partner feel the same. This last month can feel like the longest and shortest month of the entire pregnancy. All you can focus on are the last days leading up to the due date.

When are they coming? Is this labor? How are you feeling?

Every day before the due date, your mind is still preoccupied with the same expectant thoughts. You know the baby is on their way, and you definitely know by now that they're the ones calling the shots here. For now, just try and make sure all your ducks are in a row and the baby will arrive when they're ready. This month we'll also talk about a few more things to consider, especially in the delivery room and before.

It's been a marathon already but keep holding on. One step at a time.

This really is the homestretch.

"GET OUT OF ME. NO WAIT, STAY FOREVER!"

TERMS TO KNOW

Lightening / Engaging – When the baby drops lower in the mother's cervix, preparing for delivery.

Contractions – Muscles in the uterus tightening and relaxing to help push the baby out.

Effacement (ripening) – The process of the cervix stretching and thinning to deliver the baby.

Dilation – The process of the cervix opening to deliver the baby (10 cm is go time!).

MOTHER AND BABY

Week 36 and your baby is the size of a papaya (18.7 inches & 5.8 pounds/2.6 kg)! This is it, the first week of the last month of pregnancy. Maybe. Sometimes cozy babies will stay for an extra couple of weeks. In any case, the baby's connection to your partner has often really bloomed by this time.

Your partner may feel more than ready to have the baby finally be born, but also never wanting this strange feeling of connection to end. They've gotten used to the weight now—even some of the aggravations—and so they may say they "want this baby out of them" and then echo in the same breath that they "never, ever want them to leave." It may not make much logical sense, but just keep in mind that it's also perfectly natural, and it can make this entire last month, in a word, *bittersweet*.

All that said, these last weeks see the baby with fully developed muscles, bones, and digestive system. They're working on the *meconium* (they've actually been working on it for a while now)—the slimy, tar-like first poop that arrives shortly after birth!

It's a little gross, and it might be part of your first *baby poop story* (every dad has at least one), but it's also a great sign of functioning systems. Their bones are strong now, too, if still malleable, and their jelly-like muscles are ready to get stronger by the day after birth. If you get an ultrasound, you'll also see the body and the face have filled out, complete with adorable chubby cheeks and all.

During the thirty-sixth week, your baby is very likely in the head-down position and lowered into your partner's pelvis. That's great because your partner will be able to breathe a little easier (less pressure on lungs and diaphragm), but also, yikes! There's a bit more pain on the pelvic area supporting your six-pound papaya! That's a heavy fruit!

Your partner may also be noticing some increased swelling in their feet, and possibly a bit more heartburn. The best thing for swelling is shoes with a lot of room and keeping her off her feet as much as possible. Antacids might also be great to have in your back pocket (or go-bag!) for heartburn. The other thing to look out for are any changes in vaginal discharge. There's likely to be a bit more, and that's normal, but if the discharge is watery, it could mean amniotic fluid and the water breaking.

If the water breaks, most women go into active labor within twelve hours—which still really makes the rush to the hospital in the movies seem a little exaggerated.

WHAT'S HAPPENING WITH YOU - CONTRACTION TRACKING APPS

You know the stages of labor. You know what to look out for: **contractions**. However, when they start, how do you know when the stages of labor are progressing, or how fast? For this, we wholeheartedly recommend getting a contraction tracking app.

There's not much more to say about them other than that they will be vital during the stages of labor. They'll help you stay engaged with your partner during the process so they can focus on getting through those painful contractions. Some apps also make sure you know just when to load everything into the car and head to the hospital.

There can be a lot of suddenness and surprise in the early stages of labor, and it's nice to at least feel like you have a good grasp on where you are in the process. Trust us, the app will make all the difference. But also keep in mind, this app is mostly for you. Your partner likely won't like you calling out every update you have just because you have it. They're a little busy at the moment.

REFLECTIONS FROM OUR DADS

"I wish I told myself to read the manuals in the third Trimester. For some of the gadgets we bought – e.g. the formula machine - I wish I had told myself to understand how to use it pre birth as reading a manual on 1.5 hours sleep with Twins is like doing nuclear physics!"

- Adam I, London, UK.

"Talking to more established dads has been great. It's nice thinking I'm not alone on this. Since lockdown, I have to say, we seem to be better at talking as blokes. Long may that continue."

- Rob S. York, UK.

"We knew exactly when we were giving birth." My partner Amy has diabetes so they actually gave us a specific date at 36 weeks for her to actually give birth via caesarean, so it was all as controlled as possible."

- William F. Leicester, UK.

☑ WEEKLY CHECKLIST

☐ Download your contraction app to prepare!

☐ Make sure your work is aware of the baby and make plans needed for potential leave very soon.

☐ Make necessary calls to finalize a pediatrician or midwife for postpartum care.

☐ Talk with your partner about preparing a baby announcement!

PRACTICE BREATHS INSIDE & OUTSIDE

TERMS TO KNOW

Oxytocin – A natural hormone released during pregnancy that causes the uterus to contract, also stimulates milk production.

Pitocin – Synthetic form of oxytocin used to induce labor.

"Bloody Show" – Vaginal discharge towards the end of pregnancy, often the result of the mucus plug falling out or loosening.

Jaundice – Condition where the skin turns yellow, relatively common in newborns. Almost 60% experience it to some degree.

Nuchal Cord – Medical term for when the baby has the umbilical cord wrapped around their neck.

MOTHER AND BABY

It's Week 37, and your baby is now as long as a head of romaine lettuce (19.1 inches & 6.3 pounds/2.8 kg)! This week is another huge milestone because the baby is officially considered out of pre-term and has entered early-term. The big actions for them right now are putting the finishing touches on their brain and lungs.

They're still swallowing in that amniotic fluid and getting great practice for breast and/or bottle feeding, while also continuing to make literally trillions of synaptic connections. That's right, the baby is firing on all cylinders now and they are raring to go . . . well, not necessarily *rearing* . . . 97% arrive headfirst, but still.

Either way, the baby is still doing their first practice "breaths" to strengthen those lungs for a big gulp of oxygen outside the womb. That might cause some noticeable hiccups, but your partner might also be practicing breathing too (Everything we learned from prenatal classes!). As Braxton Hicks contractions can become even more common this week, it's likely your partner is doing a few of those breathing exercises to center herself and prepare for the real thing.

The other big thing for your partner this week is the cervical mucus plug is likely to drop out. You remember way back in the first trimester when that plug protected the uterus from bacteria? Well, since it will now cause a traffic jam for delivery, the cervical plug falls out with a relatively bloody discharge, either all at once or some at a time.

YOU'RE GOING TO BE A DAD!

In some truly poetic naming conventions, this is called the "bloody show."

We know, it must've been Shakespeare or something. This bloody discharge can cause alarm for most moms-and-dads-to-be, but rest assured, it's natural—the baby is not more susceptible to infection, and it means they're about ready to arrive!

However, the bloody show is not the only thing to look out for this week. Your partner might also be feeling continued pressure in their abdomen, and possibly some new stretch marks. Try your best to lather them up with belly oils and butters, give them massage, and encourage them to lie down as much as possible.

WHAT'S HAPPENING WITH YOU - BIRTH EXPECTATIONS VS. REALITY

It's likely been in the back of your mind for months, but as reality starts to get nearer, what *exactly* has been in your mind with regards to the delivery, your partner, and your baby? Has it been a glorious, valiant moment of you carrying your partner to the car, holding their hand as they gently exhale when the doctor says "it's time to push," and dabbing glistening trickles of sweat from their forehead? And then, after a couple of brief minutes of cinema-worthy pushing, backed by a triumphant orchestral score, the doctors nod to you in a resolute sort of way and reveal your perfectly cleaned baby ready to be held, crying, but *not too loud?*

That fantastical view of the delivery room isn't shared by every first-time dad, but we can all get lost in daydreams sometimes— and that's okay. However, it's still good to squash some daydreams outright. Don't get us wrong, the birth of your baby is still a magical moment, but it's magical because of its reality, imperfections, and grossness—not because it's the perfect scene from a movie.

First, be prepared that your baby might not look like what you're imagining. When they first come out, their head is likely to be slightly cone-shaped from squeezing through the cervix and vaginal canal. Their eyes will be puffy and bloodshot, the cheesy-looking vernix will likely be covering their bodies, and their genitals will likely be swollen. They also might have jaundice (a yellowing of the skin), or perhaps whiteheads, birthmarks, bruises, and possibly a rash. Eventually, they'll look far more like you've daydreamed, but probably not right at the beginning.

We've already gone through the stages of labor, but the reality of it is far more challenging than reading it. Most women's labor can last anywhere from four to eight hours, but some women can be in labor (even past the early stages) for a day or more. And that time can be exhausting, sleepless, and anxiety-filled.

However, there are more things to be aware of upon delivery. It's extremely common for women to poop during delivery—after all, when a doctor says "push," what muscles are we going to use to push besides the ones we've used all our lives?

It's also possible that your partner's vagina will tear during delivery. If it seems likely, the doctor might recommend an episiotomy—a small, controlled incision that allows more room for the baby to squeeze through. Those perineal massages we talked about before can be done to reduce the likelihood of tearing ahead of time.

If your partner receives an epidural, they will also be getting a catheter (urine tube) because they will be numbed and unable to feel when they pee, poop, or birth.

And if you cut the umbilical cord after delivery, after it's done doing its job (when it's not pulsing as before that it still contains nearly 30% of the baby's blood and helps them breathe while they're still learning too), there might be a little squirt of fluid when you do. It's also pretty tough to cut through that Wharton's Jelly—really durable stuff!

Your baby might also come out with a *nuchal cord*, where the umbilical cord is wrapped around their neck—sometimes more than once. While it isn't always as life-threatening as it seems (because the Wharton's jelly is thick and they're still breathing through that cord rather than their lungs) it can still be dangerous by restricting blood flow to the carotid artery and needs to be promptly addressed.

Finally, there's the question of where you are during the whole ordeal? *Are you standing beside your partner? Are you in the room? Are you holding a leg and watching as the doctor catches your baby?Are you holding your partner as she catches her own baby?* No matter where you are, make sure you're prepared and doing what you can to be involved, but not in the way. If you're queasy about blood, it might not be the best call to watch—and if you're not queasy, it still might not be something you or your partner necessarily wants you to see.

Then again, it also might be something you're both looking forward to.

Your only goal right now is to make sure your expectations fall more in line with the realities coming to you. Even though these realities are less picture-perfect than your daydreams or the movies, this can still be one of the most moving and amazing experiences of your entire life.

REFLECTIONS FROM OUR DADS

"I'd say to other dads-to-be to realize their sense of empowerment, even in labor. There are things that you're allowed to say yes and NO to. Know your rights as a parent. The key is trusting your partner, and understanding your rights. E.g. If you believe in things like active birth, all the stats suggest it's much better for the mother, but the convenience of lying on your back is what hospitals preach. So just be as informed for yourself and your partner as much as possible."

- Ameet H. London, UK.

"Because Sarah was carrying twins, we had a planned C-section - at 37 weeks. I have to admit, knowing the exact date and time of the arrival was a weird feeling."

- Adam I. London, UK.

"We didn't have anywhere for the baby to sleep until that last week, and we borrowed a lot from friends - they all came through!"

- Jon P. London, UK..

☑ WEEKLY CHECKLIST

☐ Make sure the baby's clothes are washed with a newborn safe detergent and ready to go! They're about to get some use!

☐ Talk with your partner about everything they'd like in the delivery room to make it a comfortable and stress-free environment.

☐ Schedule the *Group-B Strep Test* if you haven't already.

WEEK 38

READY WHEN YOU ARE

Melanin – Hormonal changes in pregnant women near labor that can change skin complexion, hair, and eyes.

Water Breaking (Breaking of the Waters) – Rupture of the amniotic sac, causing the fluid to drain out of the vagina, which means the baby is almost ready to arrive!

MOTHER AND BABY

Your baby is now the length of a stalk of Rhubarb at 19.6 inches (but weighing like loads of Rhubarb at 6.8 pounds/3.1 kg!). That's right, your baby is now weighing almost seven pounds and is nearly ready on all accounts. They've shed almost all of their lanugo (downy hairs) by now along with most of their vernix (the white protective coating) and a few dead skin cells. All of that is now mixed in a wonderful goulash of amniotic fluid inside the uterus that the baby continues to swallow until a good portion of that meconium is safely stored in their intestines. And they're keeping it there, a nice hot steamy one, just for you.

The meconium poop right after pregnancy looks a bit like tar and is just as sticky. Overall, the baby is doing everything they can to prepare themselves. Their bags are packed, their skin protection is shed, and they're ready to go.

As for your partner in these last weeks, it's tough to say. She might be relentlessly tired or have spurts of energy as she frantically nests the house and prepares for the baby's imminent arrival.

Beyond that, and possibly some real difficulty sleeping, most women are doing the famous pregnancy waddle by now. Some might have started sooner, but as the baby drops lower to the pelvic region, walking becomes like carrying a kettlebell or a ten-pound bag of cement between their legs. It gets heavy after only a few minutes, and it's hard to imagine how heavy it must feel after days and weeks. This is when the support belt becomes even more of a must and a welcome best friend.

The sentiment right now is pretty clear: "Ready when you are, baby."

WHAT'S HAPPENING WITH YOU - LAST MINUTE PREPARATIONS

At the end of thirty-eight weeks, your baby will officially be a full-term pregnancy. However, with the expected delivery fast approaching, it's time to do those last-minute preparations. For you, that might mean getting your go-bag prepared. Here's what we recommend you have inside:

- A picture ID and insurance card or information
- Your birth plan
- Essential toiletries like toothbrushes, contacts, bath items, deodorant
- Slippers and a bathrobe or nightgown for your partner (coziness first!)
- Chargers for phones, computers, other devices - Extended phone charging cord (possibly 10ft) to actually reach the hospital bed
- Entertainment like books, journals, or tablets
- Portable speaker or any way to listen to music
- Favorite snacks and drinks (if the vending doesn't have them)
- Cash or cards (for the vending machines or gift shops)
- Extra underwear
- A bathing suit (in case your partner wants to shower and needs help being washed)
- Comfortable clothes for you and your partner, plus coming-home clothes for the baby!
- And finally, baby nail clippers and a baby blanket.

All that is for you and your partner's go-bags. However, you also need to make sure you have your infant car seat installed too! If it's your first time doing it, read the instructions before you install it, and then maybe take it out and do it again just to make sure it's perfect. You can never be too careful!

Beyond all that you're doing to get ready, you might also notice an uptick in energy with your partner and, as we mentioned previously, the extreme nesting mode. They might be cleaning, organizing, putting finishing touches (and then even more finishing touches) on where the baby is going to sleep.

You might be doing a lot of the same, but even if you're not, take as many opportunities as you can to help your partner with the nesting. They may seem a little frantic in preparations but read the room as best you can and help out wherever possible!

REFLECTIONS FROM OUR DADS

"Because of COVID restrictions, I wasn't allowed in the first phase or second stage of labor, but was allowed into the maternity ward. Fortunately the final part was really quick. We left home at 01:00, and my partner had given birth by 03:30. I felt she was like a warrior."
– Ameet H. London, UK.

"I got laid off 36 hours before Ryna, my partner, gave birth! It was a shock to say the least, but it allowed me to spend more of my time with our new family. We had savings I knew we could rely on for a little while."
– Field C, Seattle, US.

☑ WEEKLY CHECKLIST

☐ Put the finishing touches on the nursery or the place for baby and everything else at home in anticipation of the newest member of your family!

☐ Do a practice run with some of your new baby gear—just to make sure you're ready to use them!

☐ Prepare a few meals and have them in the freezer (something easy to reheat and enjoy) or reach out to friends or family to have a back-up plan for food; it's just hard to find time to cook right after the birth.

WEEK 39

THE FINAL COUNTDOWN

TERMS TO KNOW

Inducing Labor – Process, whether natural or artificial, of encouraging labor to commence in order to birth the baby.

Crowning – When the baby's head first begins to push out through the vagina during delivery and you can see it.

MOTHER AND BABY

At thirty-nine weeks, your baby is now full-term and the size of a pumpkin (20 inches & 7.3 pounds/3.3 kg)! They have now reached their full birth weight and likely won't do too much more growing, which might be a relief for your partner. A small stipulation, however—even though the baby is now considered "full-term," there's still some development happening inside. Think of it like those last-minute edits or quick fixes before you finally deliver something you've really been working on—a project or a piece of art, a movie, or . . . you know, *life*.

The big developments these last couple of weeks are with, you guessed it, the brain. The brain is 30% bigger than the previous month (accounting for a third of the baby's total weight) and it won't be done growing for years after the baby is born. But besides just getting bigger, the activity going on in there is vast. It's like a big pile of laundry waiting to be folded and organized to turn into thoughts, emotions, ideas, personality, reflexes, and everything in between!

Your partner, on the other hand, is in full swing preparing for the delivery. That might show up in some interesting ways. Unfortunately, she might feel a return of lightning crotch (if it ever left), and the pressure on her pelvis is likely getting extreme. One particular way her body is preparing is through effacement (ripening or thinning) and dilating (opening up) where the cervix is doing everything it can to prepare for the baby's exit. For some women, this happens over the course of weeks, while for others it's a quick process that happens during labor.

Speaking again of labor, it might be well on the way—and it is indeed *laborious*. Labor can be extensive, but starting it up can be a process as well. Sometimes women feel like they're more than ready to get it going—and for that, there are a few ways to go about...

WHAT'S HAPPENING WITH YOU - ENCOURAGING LABOR

As we've said from the beginning, time is relative when it comes to your baby. They might show up right on their expected due date or they might show up before or after. Whether you and your partner want the baby to arrive as close to the due date as possible, the baby is already late, or your doctor has talked to you about encouraging labor—there are quite a few ways to do it naturally (even if there's a lot of debate as to how effective they are) before medical inductions are necessary or desired.

Just a heads up, yes, these are the more "natural" ways of inducing labor, so take them with a grain of salt. However, we're going to say no to the castor oil method—that's pretty much just a laxative that hasn't held up to modern scrutiny.

Walking

A lot of pregnant women have found that going on walks can help encourage labor, releasing endorphins, and possibly giving some welcome relief.

Sex

The name of the game is increasing oxytocin levels, and sex does that in spades. If it's something that's applicable to you and your partner, sperm contains *prostaglandins*, hormones that can actually help to dilate the cervix. It may be tough at forty weeks to pull it off, but hey, it's worth a shot. Also, if you're already there, nipple stimulation has also been known to encourage labor, so maybe add that to your *moves*.

Massage

The last way to encourage labor that we'll recommend—because we're still hit or miss on spicy foods and who herbal treatments like evening primrose are best for—is a good old-fashioned massage. Like sex, a massage has the opportunity of raising oxytocin levels. Pitocin (synthetic oxytocin) is what doctors use to induce labor. The only problem is, Pitocin works a little too well, often causing the woman's uterus to contract more and more powerfully than it ever would otherwise. So the more we can help relax our partner, get them cozy and comfortable, the more natural oxytocin is likely to be released to stimulate labor.

It might be trial and error to see which method works best. But once your partner is in labor, *they're in labor*—so either something worked, or your baby just decided it was time.

REFLECTIONS FROM OUR DADS

"I tried as hard as possible to keep Kirsty out of her 'thinking brain' – so she wasn't overly processing things, and could keep her focus where it was needed."

- Damian C. Tonbridge, UK.

"I usually can't stand blood, but I definitely had no trouble being right there in the action! A different kind of consciousness took over, it was very cool."

- Keith G. Seattle, US.

"We left it as natural as possible, and did Hypnobirthing alongside our own faith-based approach. She was meditating and I was mindful of her in her own space. I left that space with a whole new level of love for my partner."

- Ameet H, London, UK.

"My partner had a VERY complicated birth that meant the Health visitor was coming to our house, every day – testing us. She had an Emergency C-section, and then my wife came home and got an infection and had to go back in for 5 days. I made an agreement with midwife to have the baby back in the hospital. But it meant I could only go see her for two hours a day. I raised her mental health risk and so the hospital let them go home to help with her mental health, but the nurses came out to make sure she's ok – literally everyday. She was put on 3 weeks worth of antibiotics."

– Kristopher F, Greenock Inverclyde, Scotland.

☑ WEEKLY CHECKLIST

☐ Spend some quality time with your partner:

    ☐ Plan a nice in-home date complete with a couch picnic and a good movie.

    ☐ Go on a slow, leisurely stroll nearby.

    ☐ As long as your doctor hasn't warned against it, sex is completely possible up to delivery; just keep in mind that it might induce labor!

☐ Keep in solid contact with your doctor, midwife, or doula for those important last-minute questions.

WELCOME TO THE WORLD

TERMS TO KNOW

Apgar Score – Tests and measurements performed on newborns after birth to assess their health.

Overdue – A pregnancy that continues for longer than 42 weeks.

Inducing Labor – Stimulating contractions (through a variety of ways—sometimes exercise or sex) to start up labor and encourage a vaginal birth.

"Golden Hour" – The first hour after birth in which mothers are encouraged to spend the time holding their baby as a means of initial bonding.

Skin-to-Skin Contact – A technique where newborns are kept on the chest of their mother for a variety of bonding and physiological benefits.

Afterbirth – After the baby is delivered, the stage of labor where the uterus pushes out the placenta.

MOTHER AND BABY

Any day now and your baby is here and they are now the size of a watermelon (20.2 inches & 7.6 pounds/3.4 kg)! Or really, they're the size of *your* baby! Whatever the size, your partner can definitely feel their weight. Can you believe it? A few months ago, a poppyseed, and now this miracle of life is ready and waiting to meet you.

This week, a long road is coming to an end, and a new one is beginning all at the same time. The marathon is almost finished, the masterpiece almost unveiled. Your baby has been working hard on developing, your partner has been working hard on providing for their development, and you've been working hard to support, nurture, and help out during this entire process. But now, at last, the end of the pregnancy is here.

The baby has shed most all the lanugo and vernix, and their brain and lungs are prepared for the world. Your partner is feeling large and in charge, but also more than likely over-eager, and probably anxious, to meet this beautiful creation. There's been a tremendous build-up to this point, and it might not be over just yet. Your partner is ready, your baby is ready, *you're ready*—and this week, it's (hopefully) time for their birth.

You've got the go-bag, you know the route to the birthing center or the hospital, you have the car seat installed, and everything has been taken care of at the home you're about to bring the baby home to. Or your home is the place you decided on for delivery. Either way, you have the information you need, you've done the planning, now it's finally time to meet your baby.

WHAT'S HAPPENING WITH YOU - "YOU'RE A DAD."

Just like we said at the beginning, there are so many ways that babies come into the world. We have no idea the situation that brought you here, or what you'll experience in the delivery room—wherever that happens to be and what kind of birth you and your partner decided upon. But after all these months of challenges, anxieties, joys, revelations, moments, decisions, and that stunning mix of excitement and nerves—*you're finally here*. We couldn't guess the point at which the pregnancy and everything it represents becomes real for you, but it *is* real now.

So congratulations, because **you're a dad!**

EMBRACING THE GOLDEN HOUR

In a hurry to measure, clean, and weigh babies, some mothers miss out on the "golden hour" of bonding with their newborn. Not all mothers get this opportunity and that's completely okay too, but barring any emergency that requires the newborn in the NICU or other intensive units for immediate care, the first step after birth should hopefully be leaving the baby to their mother for immediate "skin-to-skin" contact.

This first hour of immediate skin-to-skin bonding is recommended to be a quiet, undisturbed time where the baby and the mother can basically get to know each other. Because "getting to know each other" has value both mentally and physiologically. To add, the mother is still in labor at this time because the placenta has yet to be birthed, which means the baby is still connected to her by the umbilical cord.

While waiting for the placenta to birth, the "golden hour" is where the mother has the opportunity to meet their baby, bond with them, and potentially breastfeed them for the very first time. There are quite a few reasons to ask for skin-to-skin contact and embrace the "golden hour" from your provider for both you and your partner:

Temperature Regulation

You know by now that your baby has had a number of things helping them regulate their temperature. At first it was the lanugo (downy hairs) that they've mostly shed before birth. After that they built up their brown fat stores and their brain is ready to activate them. However, inside the womb, your partner was still helping them with that process. Because of that, when they come out into their first unregulated temperature environment, their bodies will be learning on the fly exactly what to do.

To help them, a mother can hold the baby to their chest and their body can quickly help the baby acclimate to the outside temperature, and give the baby a chance to really learn how to do it on their own.

Respiration & Breathing

Your baby has been practicing breaths inside the womb for a long time now, (often with those cute little hiccups) but now it's the real deal. When they first come out, their umbilical cord is still doing what it has been doing for months, helping them to breathe. However, that cord is only a safety net anymore, because they're going to have to put those little lungs to work themselves.

When a mother can hold their baby immediately after birth, their voice can soothe them as they rub their back to try and coax that first breath and possible first cry outside the womb. Babies often have quite a bit of amniotic fluid stuck in their throat which a mother can help them to get out to encourage the first breath, alongside any doctors' instructions.

Delayed Cord Clamping or Cutting

As mentioned, the umbilical cord is the baby's lifeline. When they are born, it's very often still hard at work to help them breathe and supply them with blood and vital nutrients. If the cord is clamped or cut before it has stopped pulsing blood, the baby can experience a harder time with those first breaths and could have a low birth weight as 30% of their blood (a fair amount of ounces) was still being pumped.

So as important as it is to get those Apgar measurements, most of them can still be done while the baby is safe on the mother's chest.

Hormone Rush

Pregnancy hormones have been a common theme throughout the pregnancy, but immediate skin-to-skin contact after the baby is born and simply smelling the baby often brings about a slew of new oxytocin activity in the mother's brain. This hormone promotes a connection between the baby and the mother and helps with bonding. You actually experience a similar thing with skin-to-skin bonding with your baby as your brain also produces that oxytocin— more on that later!

To add to the oxytocin rush, prolactin is also created with skin-to-skin bonding which is the first milk that can be offered to the baby through breastfeeding. Even if breastfeeding isn't part of the plan, the hormone still helps with initial bonding. It also helps to encourage the baby.

Protects Against Separation

When a baby is born, they naturally want to feel in a safe environment or somewhere familiar, and to them, that's with their *home*—their mother. Because of that, taking a baby away from their mother immediately after birth can often cause some extreme reactions (a lot of crying) as they are away from their source of safety, nourishment, and heat.

Although not every mother will be able to experience the "golden hour" with their baby and, again, that's completely okay (there is **plenty** of time to bond)—if it is possible, it's heavily encouraged. And that also brings up where *you* are during this time.

Hopefully, you're right by both of them.

As a dad observing the hour, being close enough to your partner and your newborn might have your own surge of oxytocin, and that surge can be immensely rewarding and help facilitate your own unique bond with the baby and even your partner. We'll get more into that a little later, but for right now, after the "golden hour," hopefully you have the opportunity to hold your baby for the first time too!

The "second golden hour," as we like to call it (or however much time you can get) is a great starting point to building your brand-new relationship.

Just as skin-to-skin contact is important for the mother and baby, the same can be said for you. It can encourage that oxytocin release as we mentioned, but smelling their hair or being nearby can have a similar effect. But it's a mutual benefit, because as much as it helps you connect with your baby, just holding your baby can help them too.

They might be used to your voice from the famous "dad storytime," and hearing that voice can be calming to them in this new world they're experiencing. It can give them a sense of comfort, helping them to calm and even improve the quality of sleep.

REFLECTIONS FROM OUR DADS

"It was so strange to be at the hospital during labor. Because of the restrictions they wouldn't actually let me stay in the same room as my wife, but they would let her walk around and me too. We would secretly meet in the elevator just to see each other and ride up and down a few floors together, just to have time. The craziest part is that we weren't alone in that. Many other couples did too."

- Jan T. Warsaw, Poland.

"We spent 5 days in hospital, and I had so many questions in that time - how to get her to breast feed. What do you do once she's fed...? How to burp? Should you rock, should you shush, or let them self soothe? In a way you need to go through those anxieties first to form your gut instinct."

- Damian C. Tonbridge, UK.

" I remember the very first second of seeing my daughter - she came out blue with white residue. I remember Amy and I just crying and holding Mica. It was so emotional."

- William F. Leicester, UK.

"With my first, everyone was there to visit. Family, friends, the dog. People were fighting just to see the baby. Then with my second and COVID, nobody was there. I had to cut a deal with the security guy just to escape and get some McDonald's. But the whole thing just felt sterile. Not even in the literal sense, of being in a hospital with HEPA filters, but we were there to do a job. Have the baby, leave. It was private, even intimate comparatively. There were no distractions. I even watched my son come out; I was fascinated. I'm not particularly religious but it was amazing, just--I couldn't believe it and I totally see it as the miracle of birth now."

- Barrett E. Chicago, US

"I assumed I would have an easier time with some of the transitions than I have. A lot of people said as soon as you see your baby it would be instant love. To be honest, it was much more of a gradual, growing-into-it process."

- Field C. Seattle, US.

"I could only see my child 2 hours a day. With a mask on, and then I was told to leave. The set up needs to be better. Even one where dad can't come and go but has to stay in one place would be so much better."

- Kristopher F. Greenock Inverclyde, Scotland.

☑ WEEKLY CHECKLIST

☐ Hold your beautiful new baby!

PART FOUR

THE FIRST
YEAR

YOU'RE GOING TO BE A DAD!

In the first year of your child's life, you're going to learn on the fly exactly what it means to be a dad. Your baby is going to grow, move, roll, cry, crawl, eat, poop, sleep, smile, and laugh—and you're going to be amazed each day when they make new connections in the world that they hadn't before.

New developments will happen. Their brain will literally double in size, and milestones will be there to help you understand the natural stages of your baby's growth. As we mentioned in the beginning, these next chapters won't follow the week-to-week structure that the pregnancy did. Instead, we'll focus on some of those major milestones you might experience by breaking this year down into The *First Few Days, The First Few Weeks, Months 3-6, and Months 6-12.* From newborn to early toddler, you'll be able to read along as you watch them experience this great big world for the first time.

But as you care for them and watch them grow, you might also sometimes feel overwhelmed at the awesome new responsibility that rests so comfortably and safely on your chest. Your partner will need almost forty days on average to heal from the pregnancy, and during that time, a lot of work can fall on your shoulders.

As your partner heals, breastfeeds, and tries their best to get back to how they felt before pregnancy—you'll be learning the ropes of feeding, changing diapers/nappies, adjusting to circadian rhythms, and finding time to bond. You might feel an immediate, lightning-strike connection to your baby, but you also might be too concerned for their safety and security to consider these strong emotions just yet.

Don't worry! Over the course of this first year, you'll develop a bond with your baby that is unique and uniquely unbreakable. *You're their dad*. You're the one they'll come to count on to help them and to love them. The first year starts at your baby's first breath outside the womb, and it's going to be among the most rewarding, challenging, and wonderful years of your entire life.

Let's get it started!

THE FIRST FEW DAYS

TERMS TO KNOW

Baby Soft Spots – Two soft spots on the head, also called *fontanels*, that allowed the baby to push through the birth canal; they are spaces between the bones of the skull that have not fused yet. The smaller spot at the back usually closes at around two to three months.

Breastfeeding – Also called nursing; the action of feeding the baby with milk from the breast.

Breast Engorgement – When breasts become overfull of milk and feel swollen. Usually occurs when a mother makes more milk than the baby uses.

The first few days with your baby could be spent in any number of places. They might start at the hospital or the birthing center before moving to your home. Or they might all be spent at one or the other. But no matter where you spend those first days, you'll be spending them as close to your newborn baby as possible—uncovering a whole new world as a first-time dad as they discover this one as a first-time human.

You're likely going to experience your partner trying to breastfeed for the first time, and you're going to see the toll the pregnancy has taken on her body as she works to rest, recover, and heal. You're going to hear a lot of crying and come to understand that crying is a baby's language before they can speak. There will be different types of cries that you'll begin to interpret and react to, almost like a second sense. It might take a few days, weeks or more as the *Baby-2-Dad Translator* can sometimes get lost on delivery. But don't worry, it's on the way!

You may start to be amazed by some motherly instincts that your partner just seems to have naturally. And you'll also begin to realize what fatherly instincts you have. It might be instincts of protection, of security, a desire to help—and those initial worries might prevent you from making an emotional connection or bond with your baby right off the bat. You might feel that you have your guard up but not understand why. Not from the baby, but from the whole world that surrounds your baby.

That can impact your brain in strange ways.

You might be doing that nice 25 mph drive home, you might be cautious of every family member that gets too close, you might be worried when anyone but you or your partner carries them. The important thing about these instincts that are just waking up inside of you is that they're all **born out of love.** You may not immediately feel that bond, but you might already find yourself treating this baby as the most sought-after treasure in the entire world—because to you, they are. They're becoming *your world*.

YOUR BABY

After all those comparisons to fruit and vegetables throughout the pregnancy, your baby has arrived. On average, your baby will be somewhere between six to eight pounds (2.7 to 3.6 kg) and fairly close to twenty inches. However, it's also extremely common that in the first few days, your baby loses about 10% of their birth weight. Don't worry, it's completely natural.

But it does bring up the *first of the four* biggest aspects of those initial days: *feeding*.

The Basics of Feeding

Whether formula or breastfeeding, a newborn baby feeds quite literally around the clock. Just imagine, they used to have instant access to nutrition and food—that's a daydream for you, an instant food dispenser while you relax on the couch with a good film. Ahh, lovely. Even if your partner wasn't eating, they were still absorbing what they ate last, whenever they wanted to. Now that they're out in the world, your baby will likely be hungry every **two to three hours.**

During the feeding times, it's really all about assessing your baby's cues.

Are they still hungry?

Do they need to be burped?

Is the formula or milk too cold?

All babies are different. Some might need a little coaxing to eat, some might latch on to the breast or bottle immediately. Don't worry, you'll come to know how they feed, and you'll learn a few tricks only applicable to your baby. Working with averages, a baby on formula will need about **two to three ounces (60 to 90 ml)** at feeding time. You'll also need to be sure you sanitize before every use.

On the other hand, a breastfeeding baby will typically let your partner know in their own way if they're still hungry. If the first breast gets soft and quite literally sucked dry, they might want to move to the other—and your partner will likely alternate breasts each time anyway. The more milk your baby drinks, the more your partner will produce—and it typically takes a while to get on a good supply-and-demand cycle for that. On average, a breastfeeding session can last anywhere between **twenty and forty minutes.** Sometimes less, sometimes more—but again, that all depends on your partner and the baby.

But after all that feeding, how can you make sure they're getting enough food? Well, that's the next aspect: *bladder and bowel movements.*

The Basics of Bladder & Bowel Movements

A baby is going to poop and pee **a lot**. As it happens, breastmilk and formula seem to work a lot like coffee. They'll be going through anywhere **between five and eight diapers/nappies a day.** That's a good thing though! Their digestive system is getting a test run, and they're learning where to send those nutrients. The bowel movements and pee habits might be different, but one of the few causes for concern are if they're *not* happening. If your baby is constipated, definitely make a call to your doctors before trying to solve it yourself. And after a nice feed and diaper/nappy change, often a baby is ready for their third favorite thing: *sleep*.

The Basics of Sleep

Babies are a lot like lions in that they sleep a vast majority of the day. Newborns, on average, will sleep **14-17 hours** every 24 hours. But because a baby's circadian rhythm was adjusted to your partner's, they were often asleep when your partner was active, and active when your partner was asleep.

You've probably heard it from any number of people when you mentioned you were expecting: "Say goodbye to sleep!" And then they chortle to themselves as they walk away. As much as we'd like to reassure you, it's a difficult thing to predict and it's much better to be prepared for the worst-case scenario. Babies don't have alarm clocks, and their circadian rhythm wasn't based on day and night like ours.

For them, it's all the same until it isn't.

With that in mind, your baby might take a while to get adjusted to sleep schedules. And as they're getting adjusted to theirs, you're getting unadjusted to yours. As mentioned, a baby will want to feed once every two to three hours—nighttime doesn't change that. Further, it's not only the feeding, but the changing too. For whatever they need, a baby is going to cry to let you know and you'll wake up to solve the problem.

Whatever the problem happens to be, they're dependent solely on you and your partner right now. So while they get their bearings in this new world, you're going to be awake to see it—at any and *all* hours of the day and night. Don't worry, this stage won't last forever, but we have to be honest that it will be tough while it goes on.

Another thing to keep in mind is **where and how will your baby sleep?**

There's obviously a lot of options for *where*, but the essentials of *how* are often recommended that your baby should be laid down on their back, not their tummy or their side. A baby cannot lift their head, so having them face down could cause them to suffocate and result in *sudden infant death syndrome* (SIDS). For the same reason, the mattress or pad that they are laid on shouldn't have a lot of loose sheets. Try not to worry too much, however. There are a number of items on the market to track a baby's heart rate throughout the night and alert you to sudden changes—and to add to that, a baby can still turn their neck. They can't lift it, but they can turn it naturally if they're suddenly not getting enough oxygen.

So that's the basics of *how*, but as for *where*, you've likely prepared a crib, Moses basket, or bassinet (whether directly beside your own bed or not). Most doctors recommend the safest place for infants to sleep is right beside your bed in a cot, Moses basket, or bassinet. By having them close by at the beginning you'll be able to react to any crying and your partner will be close enough to breastfeed more easily. At the same time, it's also important to mention *co-sleeping*. Co-sleeping is when the baby sleeps in the parent's bed with them. While not everyone is comfortable with co-sleeping, as it increases the risk of SIDS from 1 in 1,500 (baby in their crib) to 1 in 150, it's still a fairly common practice. We won't try to sway you one way or another, it's just important to know the statistics and base your decision on what you're comfortable with.

Beyond the practicalities of sleep, something else to keep in mind is your baby's temperature. They still can't regulate it by themselves so you're going to want to bundle them up to make sure they stay cozy, warm, and minimize fussing from fluctuations. Another reason to layer the clothes is because, again, a newborn really shouldn't have a loose blanket on them, as it might suffocate them if they move the wrong way and can't lift their neck. Swaddling is still perfectly acceptable, but many doctors recommend some free movement for the baby's arms and legs (less of a straitjacket level of tightness). To add to that, it's still a good idea to remove all sheets and comforters, maybe even larger plush toys, from their sleeping area.

However, as we said, although your baby is sleeping a ton, it likely won't be all the way through the night. They'll wake up hungry or in need of a diaper/nappy change, and that can have a real effect on your own circadian rhythm—hence the frequent newborn exhaustion you might have heard about.

And this also brings up the final aspect: *communication*.

The Basics of Communication

To communicate, your baby is going to cry. At this moment, it's the only thing they know how to do to get your attention. There will be different cries for different issues that need your helpful hands to fix, but there will be A LOT of them. If your baby is hungry, cold, hot, happy, sad, or living with a full diaper/nappy—they'll cry.

It's a bit limited in the communication department, but it definitely gets the point across. Remember, crying is *all* they can do to communicate right now, so don't take it personally. It sounds strange, but a lot of first-time dads do. The baby might not fuss when your partner holds them but start fussing when you do. You wonder, *why?*

Am I doing something wrong?

In the first few days, your baby is learning about you just like you're learning about them. There might be some stepping on toes on this dance floor, but you'll find each other's rhythm eventually. Just let the music play. The only time to potentially be more worried is if the baby isn't just crying, but wailing at a much higher pitch than usual. That's when they may be indicating pain or other discomfort.

YOUR PARTNER

For the first few days after giving birth, your partner may feel like their entire body is an open wound. Not only will their vagina be sore—her muscles everywhere have been stretched, worked out, and more. We told you pregnancy is like a marathon; well, your partner's body now feels like the day after running one. Only *worse*. In fact, where the placenta was attached leaves an actual open wound, one that needs ample time to heal. As it does, she might also be experiencing *lochia*, or a vaginal discharge that is very reminiscent of a heavy period.

As she's healing, she'll likely be exhausted, as the body is putting all its energy toward recovery. Her pelvic floor is trying to restore itself, and that might make peeing a real challenge. Some women experience pain or a lack of an "empty" feeling when urinating—like they can't get it all out. Further, some women worry about their first poop after the pregnancy because they're worried about any added stretching or the possibility of new (or additional) hemorrhoids.

If your partner is breastfeeding, they'll now be hungrier than ever as they need a monstrous supply of nutrients to fill themselves and the baby. Their metabolism is at an all-time high from the pregnancy. Not to mention, breastfeeding can often be painful for many women. To add to that, she might be dealing with *postpartum depression* (PPD). We'll go into that more a little later, but for now, just know that she'll be doing her best, but she's really been through the wringer—and it can feel like the bout hasn't finished yet.

There will be plenty of things with your newborn to be happy about, but don't be surprised if your partner just seems too exhausted to share in that positivity. Whatever you can do to lessen her burdens or pressures, it will be greatly appreciated. These first days are still about being your partner's advocate, doing your best to read how they're feeling, and doing your best to help. You may both be tired, but you're still a team.

Your Partner's Possible Recovery Symptoms & You

There is no shortage of possible symptoms that your partner might be feeling after birth, and we made a quick guide of what you can do to help with each one. Above all else, your partner needs rest, and that might make them couch-locked for a while. Do whatever you can to encourage that rest, but we know you're tired too.

Head

Hot flashes
Dizziness

YOU'RE GOING TO BE A DAD!

Loss of appetite
Acne
Broken eye capillaries from pushing
Hair loss

Breasts

Soreness
Engorgement
Cracked nipples from breastfeeding

Stomach & Pelvic Region

Acid reflux
Abdominal cramping
Vaginal pain and discomfort
Lingering contractions
Difficulty urinating
Bloody discharge
Constipation
Hemorrhoids
Nausea
Gas
Incision pain from C-Section

Hands & Feet

Hand numbness or tingling
Aching limbs
Swollen or elongated feet

WHAT'S HAPPENING WITH YOU - A WHOLE NEW WORLD

You've already filled your phone with pictures and videos. You ask your partner how they're feeling constantly. And more often than not, you find yourself just watching your baby. Watching them move, shift, crack open their eyes, inhale through their little nostrils. Puffy eyes, swollen cheeks, crying or sleeping or moving and making those tiny, perfect little noises.

You bring them back home, snug safely in their car seat (that you are now an expert at installing and disassembling), and people behind you honk as you crawl 25 mph in a 55 zone. *What do they know?* You've got precious cargo. And it's official now, **you've entered a whole new world.** At the moment, it still might feel like a blur. It might be strange with all the new routines and lack of sleep. Waking concern, restless nights. You might feel disoriented. Happy and relieved, but disoriented.

These first few days after the birth are a whirlwind, to say the least. Sometimes you're thankful to see friends and family, but other times you'd rather just be totally alone with your new family. Because for many of us there's still that point. That first moment where it's just you and your partner and your baby, and you wonder: "Am I ready for this?" You leave the hospital, or the midwives leave your home, and it's just you and your partner, and the safety net you had suddenly is gone.

"Am I ready for this?"

You are. *Everything comes in stages*, and you're ready for this stage.

YOU'RE GOING TO BE A DAD!

In these first few days, you might be taking on a lot of new responsibilities. As your partner is focused on recovery and possibly breastfeeding, you're focused on everything else. You'll be waking up to change diapers/nappies, doing a lot of the work around the home, and keeping everything moving forward—one step at a time.

But more than responsibilities, it's important this week to find time to start to try and connect with your baby. If possible, this is the week to clear your schedule. We hope you've been given at least two weeks of paternity leave, but take any time you possibly can. It might feel like your partner has a natural connection, and she might, but you'll have one too. To bond with your baby, spend time with them. Allow them to rest on your chest, rock them in a chair, hold them, nap with them, feed them if you can.

When they're awake for those few hours a day, talk to them.

Ask questions, tell them about your day and the pregnancy, and how you imagined them each month. Tell them how you thought about them each day. Even if you don't feel that connection right away—because you're still in protective mode, or you're nervous about their safety—that's okay. It'll come with time. Right now, just live and enjoy being in this present moment as a dad.

REFLECTIONS FROM OUR DADS

"It's just so bizarre. You're given the baby, and you're looking after it in the hospital, but then they pack you up, and send you out with the car-seat to the Uber. You instantly go from two midwives, a completely attentive hospital, to out the door and it dawns on you that when you leave there's no longer a safety net. That support network you had suddenly just...evaporates. Thank goodness the Uber driver actually helped me strap in the baby. If it helps, the second time around is much more relaxed."

- Alex M. London, UK.

"I loved our baby from the get-go, but I didn't really bond with him until he was around eight or nine months. Since there, our bond has become incredible."

- Keith G. Seattle, US.

"One moment of horrific guilt in those first days was when I cut her finger nails for the first time. They were so soft and thin that I hadn't realised I was actually cutting into her skin and I made her bleed. I felt so so terrible!"

- Damian C. Tonbridge, UK.

"At the hospital I felt myself in true helicopter dad mode. Like a kid with a goldfish, eyeballs glued to fishbowl. I wanted to capture every breath and every moment with brain, and get all of it. But the world suddenly can seem dangerous in that protective mode, recognizing every potential hazard. Slowly that ebbed and I loosened my grip. Then you strike the balance: love and keep them safe."

- Mason C. Maine, US.

"I spent so many hours worrying about her breathing. After taking in amnioitic fluid for nine months their bodies get used to breathing at a different rate. I kept checking in on her and asking myself 'Are you breathing, I can't see your chest moving?' I'd go check on her 3-4 times per night."

- Ameet H. London, UK.

"The first time the baby fell asleep in my arms — was the first moment of really serenity and beauty."

- Robin L. London, UK.

☑ CHECKLIST

☐ Spend all the time you can bonding with your baby.
    ☐ Try to have skin-to-skin contact, resting them on your chest.
    ☐ Talk to them, about anything and everything.
    ☐ Feed them, if applicable.

☐ Pay attention to your baby's breathing pattern.
    ☐ Many doctors will say that any fewer than sixty breaths per minute is considered normal, as is a roughly six-second gap between breaths.
    ☐ If you have any added questions about breathing patterns or concerns, reach out to your doctor for advice!

☐ Learn the ins and outs of sanitizing bottles, cleaning your baby's nose (great suction tools available), and changing diapers/nappies.

☐ Remainder of the umbilical cord might fall off this week. It used to be common practice to pour alcohol to prevent infection but now most all doctors recommend doing *nothing at all* but waiting for it to fall off!

☐ Schedule your follow-up postnatal visit with the doctors.

☐ Stay observant of how your partner is feeling.

☐ Write things down, journal, and take tons of pictures or videos!

☐ Sleep as much as you can!

MILESTONES TO LOOK OUT FOR

As a quick disclaimer for milestones. Even outside the womb, your baby is still growing and developing at their own pace. None of these milestones are meant to be medical advice or standards that a baby must achieve for proper development—they're simply averages taken from data over years of study that give us a good estimation of what to look out for. So as with every standard and measures, take milestones with a grain of salt.

- Gains about 2/3 an ounce per day (after the potential drop off in weight).

- Breastfeeds 8-12 times or formula 2-3 hours per day! (& burps).

- First bowel movement of meconium!

- May briefly focus on you or your partner's face when being held.

- Sleeping like a lion! (14-17 hours per day).

somehow, their epiglottis will block the passage of the lungs so they aren't able to swallow water.

Swimming Reflex – Also not that we're recommending it, when placed on their tummies in water, babies will frantically move their arms and legs, giving the impression that they are trying to swim.

Avoidance Reflex – With the baby lying down, you can move your hand slowly toward their face (possibly holding a toy.) They will turn their head side-to-side and close their eyes trying to avoid it. This is a self-defense measure.

Plantar (Foot) & Palmar (Hand) Grasp Reflexes – Gently brush the bottom of your baby's foot or the palm of their hand. They will grasp your finger or curl their toes. It's an evolutionary relic from gripping a mother's fur. A newborn's grip is actually strong enough to hang from a pull-up bar—BUT DON'T TRY IT.

Most of these reflexes go away as the baby continues to develop. By around six months, all of them will be gone either by conscious development or lack of necessity. However, the fact that they exist at all show that your baby is actually more suited for survival than they seem to be at first glance.

That said, they still need your help constantly, and in these first few weeks, you'll start to recognize many of their developing habits. They might start to *cluster feed*, or feed more frequently than you and your partner might be used to. It's completely normal, and if it happens during the day, the baby is more likely to sleep through the night. Sweet relief!

Additionally, you're going to see a lot of the baby trying to figure out just how their muscles and bones work. In that way, it becomes your job to help.

Tummy time is something most doctors will recommend for a short amount of time. Take five minutes (which can feel like an eternity for the baby) where you place them on their tummy and have them teach themselves to lift their head and push up. At first, it's very likely their head will simply fall forward and press into the floor. But after enough practice, likely more than just the first few weeks (more likely 2-3 months), they'll be able to lift it. In the meantime, however, it may be hard to watch them struggling, but with enough time in small increments, they'll get the hang of it.

Another thing to keep in mind is how the baby sleeps. Babies sleep on their backs, but some doctors recommend to rotate their head from side to side every so often to prevent them from getting a flat spot (plagiocephaly), as their still soft skull starts to harden and fuse together.

In these weeks, you'll also likely experience a lot of firsts. The first time they focus on you, the first time they recognize your voice, and maybe even that first perfect baby laugh. No matter which first you encounter, and in which order, it always feels amazing to see how your baby is developing physically and mentally—connecting to you, your partner, and the world even more.

YOUR PARTNER

As your baby goes through a number of developmental changes, your partner will continue to heal and go through changes as well. This may have her feeling like her old self again, but there's really no way to know how your partner will react to having the baby. As we mentioned earlier, one of the most common problems for new moms is postpartum depression (PPD).

The important thing to remember is that PPD is a medical condition. Her body and hormones have fundamentally shifted and are once more trying to find their balance. In addition to that, she is likely dealing with limited sleep, anxiety, and all the things you're dealing with yourself with a new baby in the world.

Often PPD requires medical attention and possibly therapy. Some symptoms of PPD are that the "baby blues" just don't get better. She loses interest in things she once enjoyed, she has trouble making decisions, she worries or critiques herself as a mother, she suffers from insomnia, or the most extreme symptoms being thoughts of harming herself or the baby. If you notice these feelings with your partner or she expresses these thoughts to you, reassure her that they aren't her fault. The best thing you can do is your absolute best to support her and help her get the support she needs. In small ways, help her to engage with new activities, with friends or something relaxing that she enjoys. Help her regain a sense of normality with this *new normal*.

The symptoms of PPD might also cause severe mood swings that can cause her to get stuck in a depression she just can't seem to get out of. The important thing for you during this time is not to take these outbursts or feelings personally. She's likely battling inside, and she needs support more than added stress. As we said before, contact your health provider for guidance and further assistance.

In addition to symptoms of PPD, she also might start having hair fall out more regularly. Although during pregnancy, an overabundance of estrogen may have had your partner's hair looking thick and shiny, the steady decline of estrogen levels after birth can have the opposite effect—which might scare her. If that's the case, maybe try to find her a headband if she consents to the gift and reassure her that these problems won't last forever.

REFLECTIONS FROM OUR DADS

"Due to citizenship issues and lockdown it will be almost two years since Amaia was born, and I can count on my fingers the amount of time I've spent with her. My partner is from the states, and when she was pregnant I applied for a visa for them to come over. Proving there's a place they can stay, and a salary. I needed continuous employment, which then got affected through furloughing. It's been such a roller coaster!"

- Ziko T. Surrey, UK.

"The lack of sleep leads to everyone feeling a bit on edge, and it wasn't long before I realized - 'you're not going to have any time now to do anything.' It was really exciting, but also quite all over the place. For instance, I remember trying to change her in the middle of the night, and too tired to move, we tried to change her in the bed. There was an explosion all over the place! The whole bed had to be changed!"

- Simon H. Stratford-Upon-Avon, UK.

"After the birth, I felt that I had to be nurturing to not just the baby, but my wife as well. The small things added up though; say hi to your partner first when you walk into a room, not the baby. Let them know "I still care about you." Then ask, "how are you doing?" All that simple stuff. But actively try not to throw your relationship to the wayside. The truth is, it takes a long time to fully recover both mentally, and physically, but those small acts function as a "psychological band-aid" while you're both healing."
- Mason C. Maine, US.

"My wife definitely went through hairless in the first few weeks. At first she thought it was just from stress, but it turns out that the normal rate of hair loss stops during pregnancy with all that estrogen (hence the thick, shiny hair!), but then all that excess hair falls out quickly once estrogen levels drop. Crazy!"
- Keith G. Seattle, UK.

"Just keep telling yourself "IT WILL GET BETTER!" For those first few weeks I just couldn't stop him crying. It was sheer helplessness in those moments. To be honest it was despair like I've never felt. But it does get better!"
- Rob S. York, UK.

"I was surprised how frustrated I got with him. The important thing is not to take out the frustrations out on the kid. If I ever felt like that I'd take myself out of the situation. Quite literally – I'd put him down in a safe place and just decompress for a moment."
– Rob S. York, UK.

Our son definitely cluster fed, and almost exclusively at night! My wife literally got no sleep beyond an hour here and there for the first few weeks I don't know how she did it!
– Keith G. Seattle, US.

" When the baby is 'Milk drunk' and falling asleep on me, Lying on my chest - everything just feels so excellent!"
– Ameet H. London, UK

"If I was getting 5 hours in a row of sleep, I felt like I was having a lot of success!"
– Damian C. Tonbridge, UK.

☑ CHECKLIST

☐ Reach out for help when you need it!

☐ Be conscious of symptoms of PPD or PPND.

☐ The first bath-time with your baby!
    ☐ Decide on using the tub, holding them, wash cloth or another applicable device.
    ☐ Typically recommended once or twice a week by most doctors with a "top and tail" motto—that means clean crown, face, and rump!

☐ Becoming an expert at grooming your baby, from diapers/nappies to fingernail clipping.

☐ Start to learn the language of crying:
    ☐ *Are they hungry? Too cold or maybe too hot? Is their bedding uncomfortable, or their clothing bunched up weird? Is their diaper dirty? Are the lights too bright for them or noises too loud? Are they burping? Are they ill?*

☐ Try your best to establish a sleep routine:
    ☐ Bathe, dress, play, maybe a stroll around the block and off to bed.
    ☐ Try to place in the crib or wherever applicable when the baby is drowsy so they learn to associate a specific place with sleep.

☐ Get your own sleep and take any time you can for your own health and wellness!

MILESTONES TO LOOK OUT FOR

- Might be strong enough to lift their head and chest when lying on tummy

- If you offer a toy, they might reach or grasp for it

- Responding to your voice or in the direction of sounds

- You might experience that first beautiful smile as they practice facial expressions

- Some 'coos' and other small baby sounds might be made

- It's possible by three months to experience that first baby 'laugh'

BABY VISION

Starts at 8-12 inches (20-30 cm) distance and gets better from there!

Newborn: Might focus on your face or your partner's during feedings

Month 1: A preference for bold color patterns, high contrast images, or black and white

Month 2: Could start to track images, following your movements and soon distant people or objects

MONTHS 3 - 6

· · · · · · · ·

TERMS TO KNOW

Colic – Severe, sometimes fluctuating pain in the abdomen caused by gas or an obstruction; can be common in newborns and causes a lot of worrisome crying.

Teething – The (often painful) process of growing in the first set of teeth.

Growth Spurts – A point of growing quickly and suddenly in a short period of time; can cause a baby to be a bit fussier or want to nurse more.

Thrush – Fungal infection of the mouth caused by yeast; the most common oral infection found in newborns.

Strawberry Hemangiomas – A red birthmark that doesn't always appear at birth but sometimes later; comes from a collection of blood vessels near the skin's surface.

Over these next months, your baby's personality is going to start to shine through. They may not be speaking yet, but you'll begin to notice their likes and dislikes. You'll see which positions they enjoy for resting, for sleeping, for sitting. You'll feel out how they like to be held and what they're most interested in looking at or reaching for—it's still probably your face! And now your face will start to become more familiar to them, making them feel even safer.

Your baby will go through a number of changes, growing by the day and becoming more active. They've probably been lying where you set them, but now they'll start to roll over, sit up, reach for things, grab for you, and start teething. That's right, those little teeth will start sprouting in your baby's mouth, and they'll be sure to let you know when they're pushing through.

Beyond that, you and your partner could be feeling any number of ways in these months. You might have already become a well-oiled parenting machine, or you might be so far behind on sleep that you find yourself dozing off at odd times and in odd places. Because of that possibility—or the overlap of work, home life, and raising a baby all colliding at once—it's important to be conscious of your mental health in these months.

There are small things you can do for both you and your partner. It could be outings to regain a sense of normality, a place in the house where you can go to unwind and shut off your brain for a few minutes, or visiting with friends or family. Your partner will likely start feeling more like she did before pregnancy as many of those "open wounds" have closed and started to heal. In that way, these months might also be the first moment to connect once more on a romantic level, but only if you both are ready.

YOU'RE GOING TO BE A DAD!

With all that in mind, there's no set timeline for when things should be happening. Your baby is going through a developmental leap, and because of that, their routine might be changing every day. That can *really* keep you on your toes. One day you've got the dad routine down pat, and the next there's a new obstacle to overcome.

Be like water, adapt your mindset to change, and you'll be ready for whatever comes next. More than that, you'll be able to enjoy it—treasuring these rare and precious moments that you only get once. Or you'll need **sleep**, whichever comes first!

YOUR BABY

This is an exciting time for your baby's development. It will be marked by an overabundance of curiosity, but there's also some wonderful things to look forward to. In these months, your baby will likely be rolling over, pushing up with their forearms to look around, picking up objects and bringing them to their mouth, and even mimicking or babbling at the sounds you make (this is their first step toward speaking).

Even though we mentioned it during the pregnancy, it's important to bring it up again: *Try not to get too caught up in the milestones*. They are effective measures and standards created by observing a lot of babies, but they weren't made by observing *your* baby. You might notice some milestones where your baby is ahead of the curve, and maybe they're behind on some others. Regardless of where they are, our primary truth holds up—**time is relative.**

In these months, your baby will be exploring the world and building a personality that you'll come to see for yourself. However, the process can be vastly different when observing one child to another. So overall, don't worry.

Stay involved, stay present, but don't make it an added stressor.

Besides these milestones, there's another important development for the baby in these months: *teeth*. Those first ten baby teeth that they grew way back in the day are starting to sprout through. So, if you start to notice your baby suddenly drooling a ton, becoming more easily irritated, and trying to chomp with their gums on literally everything in sight—**they're teething!**

Of course, you want to be ecstatic about this new milestone, but it also means they're going to be waking up more frequently and fussing or crying—often right when you were getting settled into the semblance of a sleeping routine. The first tooth usually comes in around six months, and when it arrives, it probably won't take long for you to notice. The amount of drool is simply *astounding*. At least you know your baby is hydrated!

The Basics of Teething

When your baby starts teething, you need to make sure you have a few tools to help them with the process. There are a ton out there and always new ones available, but that's only because scientists are still trying to discover something better than your knuckles or your nose—which are go-to favorites for a teething baby.

To avoid getting your knuckles or nose covered in drool, you'll want some teething toys that your baby can gnaw on just like a family dog does. Other great things are, well . . . random frozen objects. Bananas, bagels, pacifiers, all seem to do the trick. But be extremely conscious of frozen food items when that first tooth busts through— your baby isn't ready to eat those big foods quite yet, and small pieces can be a choking hazard. The basic rule of thumb, if using frozen items, they have to be **way** too large even to be considered as a choking hazard.

And after these teeth come in, you **do** need to take care of them. Baby teeth are placeholders for adult teeth, and even though they'll all eventually fall out, losing them early can impact how those new teeth come in—even distorting the shape of their mouth. That means brushing and trying not to let anything sugary stay on them for too long that might promote decay.

The Basics of Baby Food

Babies don't need water until the fourth month, but at six months most doctors will recommend the slow introduction of solid foods. Whether or not some of their teeth have started to come in by this point, this is still around the time to at least introduce them. The important thing to remember about solid foods, besides your baby enjoying them, are allergies. Always talk to your doctor or pediatrician about possible *allergens* and what to do to prevent them.

Many doctors will often recommend a *controlled trial-and-error test*. This process means introducing your baby to one new food at a time and waiting at least two to three days before starting another. After each new food, watch for any possible allergic reaction such as diarrhea, rashes, or vomiting. If any of these occur, stop feeding that food and speak to your doctor or pediatrician as soon as possible.

Feeding and Best Laid Plans

Feeding and diet are one of the first choices you have for your baby as a parent. Typical households have a baby emulate their parent's diet. The only problem is, sometimes we don't like our diet and we "want the best for our kids."

It's a common notion, and a noble one. However, being a parent also means being adaptive. It's possible you and your partner discussed exactly how you wanted, expected and imagined to raise your baby—food is just one part of that. The only problem is, reality has limitations we don't always account for.

Perhaps your baby has an allergy to something you hoped they'd like, or they just dislike it. Maybe you don't have time to prepare a dish and you have to settle for something pre-packaged. Whatever the case, the key is to be flexible with yourself. You're making the best decisions that you can with the reality you're facing.

This isn't imaginary anymore, so try to let go of those preconceived notions of what you thought might happen and just keep making small right decisions with everything you *can* control.

The Basics of Caring for a Sick Baby

Something you should be aware of right off the bat, your baby is **very likely** going to get sick. Whether it be an ear infection, a rash, or a fever—something will happen that you couldn't foresee and you'll have to care for your baby through it.

After three months, it's not something to be afraid of, but something to somewhat expect, be conscious of, and monitor. Your baby is building up their own antibodies and immune systems, and fighting off sickness is the way to do that. For example, when your baby gets a slight fever, something around 100° Fahrenheit (38° Celsius)—the fever is the body's way of heating the system to vanquish a bacteria or infection it's trying to fight off. From the get-go, it has a built-in safety threshold of what it can heat the baby too.

It will never naturally heat the baby higher than that threshold (that can only happen if exterior factors like sunlight with no A/C in a closed car were involved), but it will very slowly and carefully, bring the fever to that threshold. The threshold that rids the body of the sickness or fights it off, but doesn't harm the baby's brain. Because of that, a doctor won't often prescribe anything if that's the case, because using something like *baby aspirin* to reduce the fever will only stifle the fever for a time. Then the baby's body will autocorrect itself and shoot that fever back up faster than it did the first time. That sudden temperature upsurge is what can be more dangerous than the fever itself.

The bottom line is, your baby is born with a body ready to fight off certain infections, to train itself to fight them, and even though your baby might get sick with something in the first year—it's no reason to sound the alarm.

Just talk to your doctor, talk to your pediatrician, and move forward from there.

YOUR PARTNER

During these months, it's likely your partner will start feeling better physically. However, just because she has physically healed doesn't mean she's not still battling emotionally. Mood swings might be common, along with outbursts, despondence, and any number of other symptoms often connected, at least in part, to PPD. You might be arguing more than you had before the baby. You might find yourself not connecting as much or becoming distant with each other.

You might just find yourselves *going through the motions*.

It's fair to assume that both of you are feeling a new kind of exhaustion, but in every instance or encounter that rubs you the wrong way with your partner, try your best to take a step back rather than letting emotion charge the situation.

She is likely going through an experience unlike any she's ever felt, and as her hormones continue to reach for homeostasis, she might have trouble understanding the crazy mixture of emotions that she's feeling. Try to be patient and be as helpful as you can possibly muster. If you feel yourselves disagreeing, stay calm and cool to avoid escalating something trivial.

Sometimes something as simple as counting to five before speaking really helps. It lets you organize your thoughts better and better rationalize what she meant with what she said. It's a small tool, but an important one to keep in mind during this time.

Having conversations about the weight of all these new responsibilities can also help a lot. Talk about it. Talk about any and everything. Joke about the 'new boss' in the house. Let her tell you about all the strange things she's feeling, and share what you're feeling too. As you build more communication, and remain honest about what's happening, the better you'll be equipped to handle it all, and enjoy it all, together.

WHAT'S HAPPENING WITH YOU - BODY CHANGES, SEX, & RELATIONSHIPS

Surprisingly, there is a little bit of science to the "dad bod." During pregnancy, you might have encountered a few "sympathy symptoms," and after pregnancy, you might have even encountered some "sympathy weight."

Don't worry, there are actually a few reasons for this:

Oxytocin

We've mentioned oxytocin before, but it's widely considered to be the *love* hormone. Women's oxytocin levels boost during pregnancy, labor, and breastfeeding, which allows their brains to more easily bond with their baby. However, a lot of studies show first-time dads have higher oxytocin levels than men without kids. The correlation has some practical causation—when dads spend more time with their kids through playtime, feeding, caretaking, or general bonding, their oxytocin levels rise.

As these levels rise, and testosterone levels drop (which we'll talk more about in a moment), it's the perfect recipe for crafting your very own dad bod. Of course, it isn't a definitive that every dad will get a dad bod. But many first-time dads might see a little more belly fat than normal, some easier to grab love handles, or perhaps a little less muscle definition. All of this is extremely common.

Don't worry, don't stress.

Right now, you have enough on your plate and when you're ready to get back into your routines, workouts or diet—you will. For now, enjoy letting it all hang loose, and focus on sleep.

Brains & Gray Matter

In addition to oxytocin, our brains go through a number of changes once we have a child. This is primarily due to a hormone shift—where we start to mirror changes that occur biologically with the mother. Our brain, even down to the gray matter, starts a copycat process— thickening parts and becoming more activated in the locations associated with emotions of nurturing and empathy. That can also sometimes mean adding on some extra pounds.

Testosterone

The other extremely common thing to happen to first-time dads is a lowering of testosterone levels, a hormone that has a lot to do with mood, sex drive, and muscle building. From an evolutionary level, testosterone is often associated with helping men to have a desire to procreate. Since first-time dads have now fulfilled their evolutionary goal, testosterone levels can drop off naturally.

In a lot of ways, that can be a good thing. However, it also brings up another topic:

Sex After Pregnancy

This mixture of brain changes and hormone changes in a first-time dad can cause a bit of an upheaval in their own bodies. Not only might they be gaining weight, but the more attention that's placed on their babies, the less they might have on other interests.

One big one: *sex*.

There's a natural delay with sex with your partner after a pregnancy as they're healing, but starting back up again may not be as easy as it sounds. Possibly for the first time in your lives, neither of you might have a particularly strong sex drive.

If that happens to be the case, starting a sexual relationship back up can feel strange. You always want to be patient with your partner, but you also have to analyze how you're feeling. If it's felt like it's been so long since you were intimate that the urge seems to have dimmed, don't worry. It happens to a lot of first-time dads. If you do happen to be struggling to start up that sexual relationship again, slow it **way** down. Remove any added pressure and rekindle intimacy first.

Make sure you and your partner are laughing together. Get comfortable together cuddling and find moments where it's just you two. They may be rare, but they're important to look for. Reach out for help. Make time. Rebuild that intimacy slowly. Don't rush anything, and you'll both be back to how you were in no time.

REFLECTIONS FROM OUR DADS

"It's just wonderful to be there with my daughter—listening to her start talking, apropos of nothing, just to listen to her nonsense stories—different things she's learned and how she connects them all. A strange, random, and wonderful dot puzzle. She verbalizes her thoughts in a stream of consciousness just for the amusement. Then just holding her or my son, smelling them and pressing my nose to their cheek, treating them like a cuddly toy. There's nothing else quite like it."
- Alex M. London, UK.

"There's no time between anything anymore – the commute becomes a walk down the stairs – we just jump from thing to thing, and there's no downtime."
- Damian C. Tonbridge, UK.

"I was so stressed about being not just a dad, but a good dad. If something wasn't working, I'd question constantly why it wasn't working, and the pressure that came with that. Then I'm also thinking about my dad and how great he was - maybe I can just try and be half as good as him, or maybe I'm just the deadbeat dad. Because of COVID - that was adding all this financial pressure too on top. It all triggered my PPND."
- Royce B, California, US.

"We built a good support system, that was key. We're both in medical field, and you'd think that might give us an advantage. But without support, support we intentionally built up, it might've felt impossible. So we had friends, family, helping us when we just didn't feel we had time to even cook for ourselves. The smallest things, they did laundry for us. But those small things, they're just like grains of sand to a beach, the little things add up a lot and pay huge dividends."

- Mason C. Maine, US.

"For any dad's going through separation when their babies are born – I'd encourage you to make *them* your motivation – it takes a lot of patience – but it gives you focus for what's ahead."

- Dom S. London, UK.

"One of the main highlights for me has been seeing their little personalities being present from day 1. Not sure if that's heightened because they're two babies. I had thought babies are basically all the same, but they've both been so different from day one. Lewis is more the chilled out one, and contemplative. While Skye is more shouty, in your face, energetic, and always moving."

- Adam I, London, UK.

"Being a dad awakened an emotional roller coaster I didn't even know was possible for me. When my son was struggling to breathe one day, I just went into panic mode. He went really red and I was super worried. I later realised it was just a tiny hair from the carpet was irritating him, but I didn't expect the sheer level of panic it could trigger."
- Matteo V. Surrey, UK

"I didn't get support from friends from those that don't have kids. It really showed me who my friends are and who aren't. But on the plus side – my older brother – has been more invested in me and my daughter way more than I thought."
- William F. Leicester, UK.

"I didn't feel like I was her 'dad' initially – in how she was responding to me vs my partner or grandma. I'd send a video of myself – "Morning Amaia..." and talk about my day, and have a song playing in the background" – just general chatter to try and help build a little bond daily...even if she was thousands of miles away at least she knew who I was."
- Ziko T. Surrey, UK.

"The shift to working from home (over COVID) means I haven't missed a bath time yet in over a year. If I'd been in an office I'd have struggled to be back by 17:30 (18:30) everyday."
- Mark S. London, UK.

☑ CHECKLIST

- [ ] Begin to find your ideal routine with:
    - [ ] The Baby: feeding, sleep, changing, outings.
    - [ ] Your Partner: communication, intimacy, outings, togetherness.
    - [ ] Yourself: health, wellness, exercise, social life, work, *me time.*

- [ ] Be open to the exploration of how those routines and "modes" might change depending on who you're with—the dad, the partner, the friend, the *you.*

- [ ] Keep working to bond with your baby, and reconnect with your partner.

- [ ] Check-in with doctors and schedule any appointments recommended.

- [ ] Enjoy these special months with your new family!

- [ ] Sleep!

MILESTONES TO LOOK OUT FOR

- Starts to laugh, giggle, or babble in long chains of sweet sounds

- Rattles and multi-textured toys becoming infinitely entertaining

- May start to roll over when lying down (no more stationary baby!)

- Practicing sitting up!

- Trying to mimic sounds you make, putting random consonants together with vowels simply to build connections

- Using their hands to reach, grab, explore, and learn!

- Might start to crawl around on the floor

- Tries to put everything in their mouth to figure out what it is and dropping them to discover new sounds—quite the scientist!

- Building memories of familiar things, like phrases you say, pointing at things you name out loud, themselves, and of course *you*!

MONTHS 6 - 12

● ● ● ● ● ● ● ●

TERMS TO KNOW

Baby-proofing — The process of making your home safe for your much more active baby.

Separation Anxiety — Anxiety that occurs in a baby from the separation or threat of separation from their parents.

Weaning — To get a baby used to food other than their mother's milk or formula.

Fine Motor Skills — The ability to make movements in using the small muscles in our hands and wrists; a common milestone to keep an eye out for.

Babies learn by exploring the world with their ears, eyes, hands, and mouth—and they'll learn more about the world by hanging out with you and playing than anything else. During these months of development, your baby will be clapping, pointing, crawling, and babbling out their very first 'dadas'—or something so close that you swear you heard and your partner just missed it, *but it totally happened.*

As they grow and move toward their first birthday, their circadian rhythms will finally become in sync with yours, giving you some much-needed rest. However, they'll also likely be inching toward the very big milestones of crawling, standing up, and taking their first steps. What that means for you is the once-stationary baby is about to get a lot more mobile in your house than before—and that means babyproofing is an absolutely necessity.

At the same time, as your baby is coming to understand the world that they're in, you're also very likely coming to grips with your new responsibility as a first-time dad. With that, not only will you have to become an expert at diapers/nappies and feeding, you'll start to find ways to balance being a father and switching between dad mode, partner mode, and friend mode. And, if you can't switch seamlessly just yet, don't worry.

You're laying the foundation of yourself, again—the *new you.*

These months might also be the first ones where you're finally able to go "out and about" with your baby consistently. Of course, there wasn't too much stopping more adventurous parents from going out before, but this is still a common time to start. However, that also means it might be time to start seeing what this new world of fatherhood unfolds. As it happens, the best way to do that is surrounding yourself with other first-time dads who are experiencing the same thing. It's wonderful for your mental health to know certain problems you're facing; you aren't facing alone.

If your longtime friends are at the same stage in life as you, that's wonderful. However, if they're not, there's other dads out there in the same boat. They've got a wonderful new baby strapped to their chest or being rolled in a stroller, but theirs didn't come with an instruction manual either. Meeting other dads, joining first-time dad groups (like the DaddiLife online community!), or just having a community you can bounce questions off can be a great stress reliever. New friends can be a sounding board for your struggles, and welcoming of the small things you yourself have learned along the way.

Being a dad is an amazing part of life, but we don't all reach that part of life at the same time—so be on the lookout for the dads who are!

YOUR BABY

Months 6 to 12 are full of non-stop firsts. As your baby starts to sit up, make sounds, laugh, smile, and play—every day will feel like something new. They'll push up higher, crawl faster, play more, lift heavier things, throw them further, make new sounds and sound out new vowels, point at more things, try new foods, and show you even more of their blooming personality.

Because of that, these months can be a thrill. Not only will your baby likely finally be settling into sleeping through most of the night, which means *you* sleep through the night, but they'll be more active during the day. They'll be excited to play, and this fervor for life can hype you up even when you're exhausted.

If you work in a way which means a long commute, coming home to your baby or seeing them after being apart for a few hours can be amazing as they start to notice who you are when you enter a room. Additionally, because their immunities have been building up over the last months, you'll likely be more open to taking them out to even more places. That may be stroller walks, a nice morning out for coffee with your partner or friends, or even longer trips or even vacations! Although these months are full of more milestones than most any other, they're also the point where things are starting to feel like a *new normal*.

YOUR PARTNER

These months can also offer a welcome return to form for your partner. You were both your own people before you had a baby, and now you're discovering who you are with that baby in the picture. It will take some time to adjust, but you *will* adjust.

In these months, the most important thing to remember is what's always important: *you're a team in this*. There will be growing pains as you discover how you work best together, and there will be points where you're both exhausted. But make time for each other and make time to appreciate one another.

No matter your current situation or relationship, you've shared an experience with them that's rare and beautiful—even through its many challenges. Make sure they know how thankful you are for this awesome and amazing privilege.

And cherish sharing it.

WHAT'S HAPPENING WITH YOU - GETTING BACK TO A NEW YOU

The pregnancy might feel like a distant memory by now, or you still might think of it often. (You may already be thinking about another one! *Oh, too soon?*) However, over the course of this process, it's very likely you've changed in some way. Big or small, you may have been resistant to it, even wary of it when it was happening—but your world is different now. *You* are different now.

As a dad, you aren't the *old you* anymore. This is a *new you*.

But it takes time to find out exactly *who* that is. You'll have many of the same interests and pastimes and friends and joys and struggles, but now you'll have something else, a shift in how they're all ordered. Your priorities might not be how they were before you had a child, and that's okay—expected, even.

Don't worry if you find yourself anxious about how your life is moving forward. You're still getting your bearings. You're finding your center, and once you do, you'll start being able to organize everything around that center. That might be reintroducing yourself to favorite hobbies or pass-times you used to enjoy, or going out in search of new ones. Being a dad can sometimes be an exhausting grind. The feeding, the chores, the routine. But there's nothing else quite like it. There's nothing like watching your baby grow and learn and develop. There's nothing like taking part in their proudest moments and helping them through their most difficult times.

By helping them find out who *they* are, you're going to find out just *who* you are along the way.

YOU'RE GOING TO BE A DAD!

It'll take days, months, years, cuts, bruises, joys, and hardships—but you'll be there with them every step of the way. And by doing that, you'll discover just who that *new you* actually is. After all, we said it before, but it's worth repeating:

You're a dad, and a damn good one at that.

REFLECTIONS FROM OUR DADS

"The geology of my friendships has shifted. I don't drink with the boys as much, but they're cool with me bringing the baby around and that's pretty wonderful. It's okay for things to shift. I felt like I had no time for myself at certain points, or that I wouldn't again. I felt like everything had to be for the baby 100%. But it's not a weakness for taking time for yourself, and you're not a bad dad for doing it."

– Mason C. Maine, US.

"It's strange, life suddenly divides into pre-baby and post-baby. But I think humans are much more preoccupied with loss than they are with gain. It's lovely to have a baby, but you also notice what you're losing from having them. If no other friends are having a baby at the same time as you, your social life is inevitably going to change. I guess it just makes us more keenly aware of sacrifices— the intrinsic nature of observable loss and projected gain. Sadness attributed to that phase of life being gone. We always feel losses more acutely than gains, but if I'm honest, everything I do still feels a million times over more meaningful now. So maybe was a good time for that chapter to close."

– Alex M. London, UK.

"It can be tough, every day I feel like I should do more. Every day I feel like I didn't do enough. But I get home from work. They're at level 10 and I'm level 2 for energy. Playing dolls is so difficult with my daughter, and I don't know what dolls say to each other. And I see with my son the dolls are going to fight and I'm more down for that. But that's the thing, what I compare myself to is unrealistic. We get these expectations from like Youtube, Instagram, social media families of these dads that are literally getting paid in ads to be the perfect father, and holding ourselves to that high of a standard. We work full time, and their full time is monetizing fatherhood. I guess my point is trying to do better each day, but cutting myself some slack."

- Barrett E. Chicago, US.

"I'm in contact with my best mates a lot more. We have a couple of different Whatsapp groups for dads now –we talk about hobbies and it's just a great release. We're all dealing with these things. For instance with my friend Tom in the group - Whenever his 4 year old is being a demon – he sends a video of just his facial reaction and sends that on the Whatsapp group. Sometimes we just take stupid photos and have a laugh about it. Am I one of those guys now, I have a 'Just wait until the guys hear about this.' mindset too."

- Kristopher F, Greenock Inverclyde, Scotland

"No one would have given me an accurate depiction of life post birth. You will never be mentally prepared for it until it happens. So don't stress about it."

- Adam I. London, UK.

"You still need a vision for YOU. Of course you're still providing a life for your new family. But you still have to think what you want your life to be. You can't just focus 100% on the baby. I didn't want to be one of those people who look like they don't know anything else in life but parenthood."

- William F. Leicester, UK.

"I love it when they're both asleep on me. It's like a moment of 'This is my world and everything just feels so excellent."

- Ameet H. London, UK.

"What I've realized is that I need my time – which is why I have a therapist – as that's about me keeping my identity outside of just being a dad. You've got to fashion out that hour, even if it's every other day – just to have a bit of you time. You schedule it in. Put something in the calendar so you don't lose touch of your life beyond the baby - Make time for you too. Even if it means scheduling it in."

- Robin L. London, UK.

"There were a couple of moments where the sleep (where Goldie was waking up every 40 mins) just wasn't sustainable. We tried sleep training and that was such a difficult moment. Charlene was getting so upset that Goldie was crying, but I knew if we didn't change something we won't be able to go on. The sleep training did help a bit. But then it regressed when she got a cold. The best way we could solve it was for Goldie to sleep in the bed with us so everyone could sleep. I think it's really just a case of doing what works for us."

- Simon H. Stratford-Upon-Avon, UK.

"The speed at which things change is remarkable – he's suddenly babbling. The development phases don't feel like they last a long time at all."

- Mark S. London, UK.

"I like to expose him to as much music as possible. I started pretty much in the first few weeks, but at 6 months onwards he really started to enjoy it! It was some severe Russian piano music that got him dancing for the first time!"

- Ben B. Norwich, UK.

"The first few months have forced me into a real work/life balance discussion. I took a month off at the start which was fantastic. I was still trying to be available for work when needed during office hours – but then I started noticing the 08:30 meetings and 18:00 going in the diary – I had to be quite strict with myself and others that 18:00 is my baby's bathtime."
- Mark S. London, UK.

"As a reflection post lockdown, I've compressed my hours. So the time I would usually be driving down to work, I now have a day off. It's amazing to be giving him his lunch everyday!"
- Ben B. Norwich, UK.

☑ CHECKLIST

☐ Prepare for the developmental leaps!
    ☐ Every day brings something new that your baby will discover and the change in a short time is simply amazing.
    ☐ Continue to bond as your baby's personality starts to shine through.

☐ Find a schedule or routine for the basics:
    ☐ Sleeping: *After playtime? After dinner? In their own crib and own room? In your room? What's nap time look like?*
    ☐ Goodbyes: separation anxiety can be powerful in babies, establish a routine for goodbyes (whether off to work or otherwise) to give them a sense of security.

☐ Most doctors recommend starting to introduce solid (soft) foods at around six months.
    ☐ Keep allergens in mind.

☐ Make some time to get out there with friends or other first-time dads.

☐ Continue building that communication with your partner and your new roles as parents.

☐ Celebrate your first year as a first-time dad!

MILESTONES TO LOOK OUT FOR

- Beginning to crawl or slink around on their belly

- Learning the ins and outs of cause and effect: They drop a toy, and it makes a sound. They drop a toy on their foot, and it makes them cry. Little lessons like that happen all the time, and might show you what your baby enjoys or doesn't—those opinions start early!

- Might start to eat soft (approved by you) finger foods

- Plays with their hands and the sounds they make: clapping, waving, opening and closing

- Starts to really enjoy peek-a-boo and social games

- Working on their "pincer grasp," so be mindful of what they're reaching for

- Starting to pull themselves up on anything they find and stand— give them a soft landing pad and plan to baby-proof!

- Start to understand the words you say and observe you like a hawk—they're trying to learn from you, no matter how mundane the task. Paperwork never looked so fun!

- Start to string together their very first words—encourage more with reading and daily practice

- Teething and gumming on everything they find

YOU'RE GOING TO BE A DAD!

- Leaving the famous "path of destruction" as they move through your home, reaching for things like toilet paper or Tupperware and giving you a trail to follow

- May start to feed themselves and love doing it!

- Might just start moving those little legs and walking!

- And finally, the very first and wonderful birthday!!! Happy One Year!

THIS IS WHERE WE LEAVE YOU

It's hard to believe how fast it can all go. Slow by the day and quick by the year, you've made it. *You've made it* through that stunning mix of nervousness and excitement when you first found out about your baby, and the rush of feelings and surplus of information after that first doctor visit.

You heard their heartbeat the first time, felt their kick the first time, heard them cry the first time, and saw them smile the first time. This past year and nine months have been full of difficult days, but also some of the best of your entire life. The journey through pregnancy and fatherhood is infinitely challenging and equally rewarding.

And now you know, *you've lived it.*

So this is where we leave you for now. You have the tools and knowledge necessary to be the dad we always knew you could be. There are many more days of fatherhood to come—your entire life, if we're counting.

It's one of those titles we never lose once we have it—*You're a dad*—and we hope we've been able to help you in some way on that journey to becoming one. If we can, we'd still love to keep offering our help. For more blogs, step-by-step guides, reflections, and conversations with a community of dads who are experiencing all of this at the same time as you, check out our website at www.daddilife. com.

From there, you'll have access to all the amazing stuff we couldn't fit into one book. Join us in the journey, conversation, and community. We're happy to have you!

· · · · · · · · · ·

OUR GIFT

· · · · · · · · · ·

TWO SPECIAL GIFTS FOR OUR READERS

AS A SPECIAL THANK YOU FOR GETTING THIS BOOK, WE'D LIKE TO GIVE YOU:

HOW TO SURVIVE ON 3 HOURS SLEEP A DAY

THE SPECIFIC TIPS AND INSIGHTS FROM THE EXPERTS ON HOW THEY SURVIVE ON VERY LITTLE SLEEP.

+

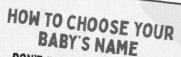

HOW TO CHOOSE YOUR BABY'S NAME

DON'T JUST RELY ON A LIST OF NAMES. LEARN ABOUT A MUCH WIDER RANGE OF NAMING TECHNIQUES TO GET TO A NAME YOU AND YOUR PARTNER WILL LOVE!

VISIT WWW.DADDILIFE.COM/NEWDADGOODS TO GET YOURS!

ACKNOWLEDGEMENTS

A massive thank you to the DaddiLife writers, Jon and Keith, for their excellent advice and edits throughout, and a special shout out to David for his countless hours of inspiration and research and 110% dedication in helping to put this book together.

A special special thank you too as always to Emilie Dorange and Jon Shortt. Emilie in particular for her design wizardry, and Jon in particular for his absolutely amazing illustrations that have brought such wonderful memories to new fathers, and wonderful throwback memories to the older dads.

We also wanted to say a massive thank you to the following organisations, with whom some of the dads we've interviewed in this book they have given us access to, or have just been fantastic support throughout:

- The Royal College of Midwives - Sean O'Sullivan and Clare Livingstone

- Deloitte - Laura Parsons

- The John Lewis Partnership - Rebecca Candy and Leanne Chalmers

- Aviva - Joe Booth, Helena Greeves, and Sarah Poulter

- Magara Law - Roy Magara

- Sooperbooks - Simon and Charlene Hood.

REFERENCES

acog.org, The American College of Obstetricians and Gynecologists

americanpregnancy.org, American Pregnancy Association

babycenter.com, Baby Center

babycentre.co.uk, Baby Centre

cdc.gov, Centers for Disease Control

fda.gov, U.S. Food & Drug Administration

flo.health, Flo

healthline.com, Healthline

mayoclinic.org, Mayo Clinic

nhs.uk, National Health Service UK

parents.com, Parents

thebump.com, The Bump

whattoexpect.com, What to Expect

womenshealth.gov, U.S Department of Health & Human Services

verywellfamily.com, Verywell Family

Printed in Great Britain
by Amazon